THE GOSPEL
Then & Now

A. M. HUNTER

SCM PRESS LTD

334 00576 0

First published in 1978
by SCM Press Ltd
58 Bloomsbury Street London WC 1

Filmset in 'Monophoto' Ehrhardt 10 on 11 pt by
Richard Clay (The Chaucer Press), Ltd, Bungay, Suffolk
and printed in Great Britain by
Fletcher & Son Ltd, Norwich

CONTENTS

PREFACE

For permission to include Part Two of this book (chapters 6–13), which first appeared as articles in *Life and Work*, the record of the Church of Scotland, I am deeply indebted to its Editor, Mr Robert D. Kernohan.

My warm thanks also go out to two Ayrshire friends, the Rev. David G. Gray and the Rev. Dr George Gilchrist, who helped me with the typescript.

Ayr   A. M. HUNTER
December 1977

PART ONE

BEFORE THE GOSPEL

I

Prologue to the Bible

How do you read Genesis 1–11, often called 'the Prologue to the Bible'?

Its contents are familiar: God's creation of the world, Adam's fall, the flood and the ark, the rainbow covenant with Noah, the re-peopling of the earth after the deluge, the dispersion of mankind after the building of the tower of Babel.

These eleven chapters, our Old Testament scholars tell us, are the combined work of three Hebrew writers, or editors, (known as J, E and P) who, using older traditions, produced their account of the world's beginnings and man's, somewhere between 900 and 400 BC.

For centuries our forefathers took these 'origin stories' with an occidental literalism: creation in six days, Adam as the proper name of the first man, an actual garden of Eden (though Eden is on no map), a walking Deity, a talking serpent, and so on.

Nowadays such 'literalism' provokes the pitying smile of men taught to think far differently by Charles Darwin and others. What we have in these Genesis stories, they say, is a collection of 'myths', and by 'myths' they mean 'pre-scientific explanations' of the world's origins and man's.

But are we shut up to a choice between these two so different views? On the contrary, there is a third approach which, it may be claimed, not only does better justice to the aim of the biblical writers, but finds perennial truth in these ancient stories.[1]

I

Let us not here spend time on the 'literalist' approach which survives now only in 'fundamentalist' circles. But are the supporters of the 'pre-scientific explanation' theory on firmer ground? We may doubt it. The biblical writers were not seeking such 'explanations'. To ascribe to them scientific leanings of this sort is to anachronize. They knew as well as we do that serpents do not crawl on their bellies today because one of their ancestors successfully tempted the first woman and her husband to their doom in the garden. So far from making childish guesses on the level of primitive science, they were reflecting on the nature of things, not as objects of scientific interest but as incidents in man's spiritual encounter with God. In short, their stories are parables, not 'explanations'.

This is not to disparage either scientific or religious truth: it is to point out the difference between scientific and what we have learned to call 'existential' truth, that is, truth about our existence in relation to the world, to other persons and to God.

Nor will it do just to dismiss these stories in Genesis as crude 'anthropomorphisms' (man making God in his own image, thinking about him in an all too human way). After all, in the gospels Christ's teaching contains anthropomorphisms, and we would never dream of calling them crude. To assume that the Genesis writers took their 'anthropomorphisms' quite literally – that they believed in a physical Deity who took an evening stroll in the garden of Eden – is quite gratuitous, and at strong variance with their profound understanding of God as the Maker of heaven and earth. (When Longinus, in his book *On the Sublime*, wished to illustrate what he meant by it, he cited the first chapter of Genesis. Here, he said, is 'a worthy conception of Godhead'.) Such an assumption springs from 'the evolutionary fallacy' which has bedevilled much modern thinking about things human and divine.

II

Now let us see how this existential approach works out when applied to Genesis 1–11.

The Prologue opens with the familiar creation story (1.1–2.4a) which many, from the Greek Longinus on, have praised for its sublimity. 'In the beginning', we are told, 'God created the heavens and the earth'; then, 'God created man in his own image'; and finally, 'God saw everything that he had made, and, behold, it was very good' (1.1, 27, 31). Here three statements are made: one, that the world exists because God exists; two, that man, unlike the other creatures, has a spiritual likeness, or kinship, to his Creator; and, three, that his created world is very much God's concern.

The second Genesis story of creation (2.4b–25) describes man's

2

place in the created world, before relating, in Genesis 3, how he fell from divine grace. Here two things must be borne in mind. First, 'Adam' is not a proper name but the Hebrew word for 'man', a human being. Second, we may say, if we will, that this is the language of 'myth', provided that by 'myth' we do not mean a fairy-tale (like Jack and the Beanstalk) but the expression in story form (i.e. parable) of something that is spiritually, or existentially, true, namely, that we humans are fallen creatures, and the story of Adam and Eve the story of us all.

Man's place on earth is set forth in Genesis 2.15: 'The Lord God took the man and put him in the garden of Eden to till it and keep it', that is, to make a home for himself and start a civilization. Free to eat of earth's wide plenty, he is subject to one prohibition: 'Of the tree of the knowledge of good and evil you shall not eat, for in the day you eat of it you shall die' (2.17). It is a reminder that man belongs to God and is under his law. To deliver him from loneliness, God then surrounds man with animals to whom he gives names. But since these cannot satisfy his need for social fellowship, God finally provides him with a human partner in the person of Eve (which is Hebrew for 'life') (2.20ff.)

Here then is a picture of the world *as God designed it to be*, and of his provision and purpose for man, the crown of his creation. Surrounded with material things for his use and enjoyment, he is given a human companion, and called to live in obedient fellowship with his Creator.

But, after this idyllic description of man's origin and primal innocence, chapter 3 abruptly confronts us with the stark reality of human sin and guilt. How man became a sinner is portrayed in the parable about the serpent who distorts, and then denies, the truth of God's threat, hinting that God did what he did for his own selfish reasons and that, by disobeying his command, the man and the woman may become God's equals. And with their yielding to this temptation, their state of innocence is at an end (3.1-13). God then pronounces his sentence on their disobedience – the toil and travail which is still our human lot – and they are expelled from paradise (3.14-24).

The story of the fall therefore teaches how self-will and disobedience defeat God's purpose for man and mar the divine image in which he was made. But all this is *parable*, not history. We do not know, nor does the Bible tell us, at what point in time (or before it) creation went awry and man took the fatal wrong turning.

Such speculations are not the Bible's interest. Its concern is the fact that, if we look around us, or into past history, man has persisted

3

in putting himself instead of God at the centre of things. The parable of the Fall is the Bible's way of saying that all down the centuries pride has proved man's downfall. 'You will be like God', says the serpent (3.5). Is not this, in essence, man's age-long temptation, namely, to run the world in his own way without regard to God or the purpose for which he made man?

Expelled from paradise, man now reaps the bitter harvest of his disobedience. With the tale of Cain's murder of his brother (ch. 4) which he tries to cover up with a lie and a denial of his responsibility, 'Am I my brother's keeper?', begins the 'Rake's Progress' story of humanity. After a genealogy in Genesis 5 comes in Genesis 6 the story of those semi-divine beings, the 'Nephilim', and their marriage with mortal women, with its dark hint of demonic powers at work in human society, before the biblical writers sum up the human situation: 'The Lord saw that the wickedness of man was great, . . . the earth was filled with violence, . . . for all flesh had corrupted their way on earth. (Gen. 6.5-11). Disobedient, lying, murderous, libidinous – so the Prologue portrays man the sinner. Is it not still a faithful picture of unregenerate man today? And if we wish further proof, do we need to look further than our daily newspaper or listen to 'News at Ten'?

Follows the story of the flood (Gen. 6.9–9.28), type of all God's judgments on the sin of man, with that of the ark as type of God's salvation. Babylonian in origin[2], this tale symbolizes the first step in God's plan to recreate sinful humanity. More, it illustrates a principle basic to the Bible, namely, God's way of saving the many by the one, or the few. (One thinks of the ten righteous men of Sodom, Isaiah's doctrine of the remnant, and, above all, Jesus the Son of man.)

Punishment of man's misdeeds by the holy God there must be, of which the deluge is the symbol. Yet, almost immediately, another great biblical truth is announced: if God's judgment is inevitable, equally so is his mercy. So, as the rainbow follows the rain, comes the offer of God's forgiveness, and the Creator makes his first covenant with Noah and his family (Gen. 9.8-17). After another genealogy in chapter 10, follows in chapter 11 the tale of the tower of Babel, (no doubt inspired by the great ziggurat, or pyramidal temple-tower, at Babylon). In origin, this may have been an 'explanation' story – an answer to the question, Why are there so many different languages in the world? – but in our Prologue it pillories the pride of man ever trying to make himself bigger than he is, as it teaches the futility of all human effort divorced from the acknowledgment and service of the one true God.

4

Such is the Prologue to the Bible when it is read as we believe it should be. William Neil[3] has summed it up:

> Man is given an ordered world and the promise of plenty. In return he must respect the natural law, namely, the equal right of his neighbours to enjoy what the Creator has provided. Thus the Biblical pattern is established: God's Judgment and God's Mercy: Neighbours' Rights and Neighbours' Responsibilities.

It is as if the Hebrew editors of these eleven chapters of Genesis wished to say to us: 'This is what man is like: selfish, proud, foolish and vicious. You know from your own experience that it is a true picture. Our business, however, is to show that that is not all. There is another side to the picture, for man is also made in the image of God ... It is not God's will that man should be the sorry product that he makes himself ... Our purpose is to proclaim God's remedy, to tell of what He has done and is still doing ... We have shown you in this Prologue the basic themes which now, in the hurly-burly of the life of a particular nation which God selected, you will see worked out in history. It is because of what we have ourselves seen and heard of what God has done for us, that we believe as we do. So ring up the curtain!'

We Christians, who regard the Old Testament as a true part of our Bible, therefore endorse the perennial truth of its Prologue. Such is man, unredeemed man, *improbus homo*, as we still know him today. But we can also point, as the men of the old covenant could not, to another and greater story, the story of how, in the fulness of time,

> A second Adam to the fight
> And to the rescue came.

Notes

1. The best exposition of this view is Alan Richardson's *Genesis 1–11*, SCM Press and Allenson 1953, to whom we are here indebted.

2. The archaeologists' discovery of a thick band of clay at Ur, Abraham's birthplace, as of the Gilgamesh Epic with its Babylonian version of Noah and his ark, shows that the biblical writers did not 'dream up' the story of the flood, though they made of it a parable of God's judgment and mercy.

3. William Neil, *The Rediscovery of the Bible*, Hodder & Stoughton and Harper Bros. 1954, p. 124.

2

God as Shepherd

(Psalm 23)

There are a few songs, sacred and secular, of which, in Shakesperian phrase, we may say:

> Age cannot wither them, nor custom stale
> Their infinite variety.

You may sing them again and again, but they remain as fresh and true and beautiful as ever. They carry a message which comes home to every generation. And so they literally sing their way down the centuries, and become part and parcel of the thoughts and emotions of men.

In the realm of secular music Burns's 'Auld Lang Syne' is one of them. In the realm of sacred music, the twenty-third, the shepherd psalm, is another. Nobody knows who wrote it, (though, as Israel's greatest king was once a shepherd, we may perhaps call it 'a Davidic psalm'); yet it has charmed more griefs to rest than all the philosophy ever written; and we may prophesy that, when Karl Marx and his *Das Kapital* are only echoes out of past history, this song of another Jew will still be sung for the comforting and enheartening of men and women in this house of their pilgrimage.

One of the secrets of the perennial charm of this psalm is its lovely simplicity. There it lies couched in words that the humblest mind can, in some measure, understand. And yet, to get the full virtue of it, we must ever remember that this psalm comes to us out of the ancient East and needs, for its full understanding, some knowledge of a way of life which is strange to us who live West of Suez. Let us take another look at the time-hallowed words.

I

'The Lord is my shepherd: I shall not want.'

The supreme question for any religion is, What is God like? With

6

what word, what image, shall we best describe the Supreme Being under whose providence we spend all our days? To one man, God is a great King: 'O Lord, thou art my God and King.' To another, he is a great Judge: 'Judge eternal, throned in splendour'. To yet another, he is a great Architect: 'When I consider the heavens, the work of thy fingers . . .'.

But to our psalmist he is best described as a great Shepherd, tender, strong and wise, able to supply his every need. When I think of God, says the psalmist, it is the image of an almighty Shepherd which fills my mind.

What does he do? 'He makes me to lie down in green pastures; he leads me beside still waters.'

Here we are to remember that in the Middle East when the noon-day sun gets hottest, the shepherd makes his flock lie down in some green hollow till the worst of the heat is over. Even so, says the psalmist, amid 'the heat and burden' of my day, God, the great Shepherd, brings me to quiet places of refreshment and renewal. But notice: an Eastern shepherd does not drive his flock; he *leads* them, walking at their head. And this, says our psalmist, is what the divine Shepherd does for me: ever before me on the path of life walks the great Shepherd, guiding my feet in the way they should go, and bringing me to green pastures and quiet waters.

'He restores my soul' (v. 3), that is, 'my life'.[1] Observe, however, that in the original Hebrew of the psalm 'restore' means literally 'turn back'; and the picture is of the shepherd 'turning back' the sheep that are prone to straggle. Just so, says the psalmist, when I tend to stray, the great Shepherd 'turns me back' and sets my feet in 'the right paths' once again. And all 'for his own name's sake' – because he is true to his nature.

Yes, but what if the road should run through the valley of the shadow (v. 4)? Even there, replies the psalmist, I will walk unafraid, for 'Thou art with me; thy rod and thy staff, they comfort me' – make me feel strong.

The 'rod' is a short, thick club, like an Irishman's shillelagh, serving as defence against wild beasts; the 'staff' – our shepherd's crook – he uses to assist the sheep in difficulty; and, so armed, he guards his flock in all dark and dangerous places where death may lurk in any shadow.

In his book *The Syrian Christ*[2] Rihbany, himself born in the East, wrote of just such a shepherd whom he had known as a boy, whose name was Yusuf.

When I think of that deep rocky gorge where Yusuf wintered

with his flock, and the many similar valleys Syrian shepherds have to traverse daily; when I think of the wild beasts they have to encounter and of the scars they bear on their bodies as marks of their undeserved and boundless devotion to their flocks, then I realize very clearly the depth of the Psalmist's faith when he wrote, 'Though I walk through the valley of the shadow of death,[3] I will fear no evil.'

'I will fear no evil', says our psalmist, 'for thou art with me.' *Timor mortis conturbat me*, sang William Dunbar, 'the fear of death disquieteth me.' But even 'the king of terrors' may be faced triumphantly if the divine Shepherd is with us in the dark valley:

> In death's dark vale I fear no ill
> With thee, dear Lord, beside me.

II

Thus far we have been thinking of God as the Good Shepherd. Now, at verse 5, the picture changes and the Good Shepherd becomes the bountiful host: 'Thou preparest a table before me in the presence of mine enemies; thou anointest my head with oil; my cup runneth over.'

'Oil' for the head, the wine-cup brimmed to overflowing – these little touches are meant to suggest the generosity of the host – of God. But why is the table spread 'in the presence of mine enemies'? Answer: by the immemorial law of the desert (and it still holds true) the bedouin sheikh is bound to afford sanctuary and shelter to any fugitive who may seek refuge at his tent-door; and while he stays there, his enemies are powerless to harm him. So the psalmist is saying, in effect, 'Keep back, all you who would harm me! God is my host and helper, and I fear not what man may do.'

So we reach the sixth, the last, and perhaps the loveliest verse: 'Surely goodness and mercy shall follow me all the days of my life: and I shall dwell in the house of the Lord for ever.'

Guidance, provision, protection, says the psalmist, have been God's gifts to me until now. His last dealings with me cannot be otherwise. Whatever the future may hold, I cannot doubt that 'the goodness and mercy' of God, like two strong angels, will be my rearguard all the way and I will be God's guest in his house[4] for ever. Or, as the old Scottish evangelist, John MacNeill, used to put it, 'The Lord is my shepherd, aye and more than that, he has twa fine collie dogs, "Goodness" and "Mercy". With him afore, and them

8

ahint, even poor sinners like you and me may hope to win home at last.'

III

Such is the shepherd psalm. It is his picture of the God-trusting life. It is as if he were saying, 'Speaking from my own experience, I have found that everything which the good shepherd is to his sheep, that has God been to me. He has led me, fed me, guarded me, and guided me. Nor is this all, for everything that the desert host is to the fugitive, that has God been to me also. He has treated me like an honoured guest, he has given me all that a guest could want. Surely then he will bless me to the very end of my journey.'

It is no wonder that this shepherd psalm is one of the dearest documents of our faith. Because of the memories it awakens, because of its association with the most sacred hours in our lives, because of its power to sound the depths of our religious longings, we can hardly ever sing it without some little stirring of emotion. Maybe our own lives have not gone as smoothly as the psalmist's; yet we cling to this psalm because it so perfectly expresses our faith in the goodness of God; because we Christians have seen – as the psalmist never saw – the Good Shepherd become flesh and blood in Jesus Christ who, for love of us, laid down his life that he might win us from our crooked ways and lead us home to God; and because that last verse speaks to us, 'in Christ', of a Father's house with many rooms (John 14.2, RSV) and the blessed hope of the heavenly hospitality of God.

Notes

1. The Hebrew word is *nephsh*, which means what you are when you are alive, not what you are when you are dead.

2. A. M. Rihbany, *The Syrian Christ*, Houghton, New York, 1916, Andrew Melrose, London, 1919, p. 218.

3. The Hebrew psalmist actually wrote *tsalmuth*, 'valley of dark shadow', but the scribal copyists pointed the Hebrew consonants to read *tsalmaweth*, 'valley of death'. Was there ever such inspired mispointing?

4. 'House', i.e. the temple. But, since in the psalm the stress falls not on the fact of the psalmist's external nearness to God but upon his spiritual communion with him, we are warranted, as Christians have ever done, in supplementing the idea of communion with God on earth with the idea of communion with him after death. In fact we have dominical warrant for so doing – see Christ's words in Mark 12.26f.

3

The Besetting God

(Psalm 139)

Centuries before Christ was born, a nameless Hebrew encountered the living God, and set down such an account of his experience as makes it one of the chief glories of the psalter.

Its theme is God the inescapable: a theme as old as Jonah who 'rose up from Tarshish to flee from the presence of the Lord', and as modern as the poet Francis Thompson who in 'The Hound of Heaven' confessed:

> I fled Him, down the nights and down the days,
> I fled Him, down the arches of the years.

Indeed, has it not been man's story all down the ages, as it is his story now? For men are still fleeing from God, and, whether they know it or not, God is ultimately inescapable.

So look again at this tremendous psalm:

1. It opens with a confrontation: 'O Lord, thou hast searched me and known me' (1–12).

2. It ascends into a *Te Deum*: 'I will praise thee, for I am fearfully and wonderfully made' (13–18).

3. It descends into an imprecation: 'O that thou wouldst slay the wicked, O God!' (19–23).

4. It ends with a supplication: 'Search me, O God, and know my heart' (23–24).

I

'O Lord, Thou hast searched me and known me.' Thus begins the confrontation. Dull must he be of soul who does not feel that these words express the most real experience of which human nature is capable. The psalmist has been personally confronted by the last reality in the universe – by the Almighty himself. He has experienced the 'I-Thou' encounter between God and man, of which the Bible is one long record. God, the 'Eternal Thou', has waylaid him in the midst of the years, and the memory of that awful rendezvous still pulsates through his words for us to hear:

> Thou hast beset me behind and before
> And laid thine hand upon me.
> Such knowledge is too wonderful to me,
> It is high: I cannot attain unto it.
> Whither shall I go from thy Spirit,
> Or whither shall I flee from thy presence?

Clearly our psalmist believed that men wish to escape from God. As they do – look at what is happening in our world today. Here both believers and unbelievers confess the same desire. They have no liking, no relish, to be searched and claimed by the power which 'moves the sun and the other stars'.

Any psychiatrist will tell you that nobody wishes to be known, to have the deepest roots of his being exposed to himself and others. And if this is true between man and man, is it not also true between man and God? From this tremendous encounter even the saints have sought to flee. For years St Augustine sought to flee God and wandered like the prodigal in the far country till that day in Milan when the voice spoke to his heart, 'Take and read! Take and read!', God's word in Christ (Rom. 13.13) came home to him, and the prayers of Monica, his mother, were answered. Or, to take a modern instance, some of us remember that splendid Christian, Tom Allan, telling how, when God spoke to him at Rheims during the Second World War, his first impulse was the same – to flee God and shirk his call.

'Be still and know that I am God' was the old Open Sesame into God's presence. But modern man shuns stillness. (Symbolic of his mood are those nose-to-tail motorists on what our fathers called 'the day of rest', or those who cannot enjoy the sea-side without a transistor blaring in their ears.) No 'wise passiveness' for twentieth-century man! His way of fleeing God is to keep rushing ahead, to be always active, always planning, ever to be conquering more and more space, or exploiting the natural resources of this planet, (and in so doing often upsetting the delicate ecological balance of nature).

But God's hand has fallen heavily on our fleeing civilization. Its flight from God has not brought it peace of mind. In its mad activism it has almost lost its soul. Its flight has proved vain.

So too, in their own way, the men of the Soviet Union try to flee God, with their official atheism, their dismissal of religion as the opiate of the people, their persecution of latter-day prophets like Solzhenitsyn, their anti-God propaganda. Yet no less futile is their flight. 'You may expel nature with a pitch-fork', says the old proverb, 'she will come back.' So it is with him who is Lord of both nature and history. For a time we may thrust God out of our consciousness, dismiss him as an outmoded superstition. But always, like his resistless tides, he 'comes back'.

Our psalmist is right. Neither in the farthest corners of the earth, nor in the hectic rush of modern civilization, nor in the pathetic godlessness of the Soviets, can man ultimately escape the God who has made us for himself and has 'set eternity in our hearts'.

II

Thus far the confrontation. Now, at verse 13, comes a change. The confrontation turns into a *Te Deum*. Before, all had been awe in the presence of the Almighty; now begins wonder at the divine wisdom. For now our psalmist realizes that even before his birth God has been at work in his life: 'Thou didst form my inward parts', he says, 'Thou didst knit me together in my mother's womb' (RSV).

Today we seldom stop to marvel at this mystery. Modern man has his own effective techniques for stifling life in the womb; and some of us who deplore the practice, save when the mother's life is in danger, are accused of employing outdated theological arguments about the sacredness of human life.

How different is the psalmist's attitude! 'I will praise thee', he cries, 'for I am fearfully and wonderfully made.' We are reminded of the character in George Douglas Brown's novel *The House with the Green Shutters* who said, 'He was a great fellow, my friend Will, the thumb-mark of his Maker was wet in the clay of him.' Just so, the psalmist pictures the Creator knitting him together, bones and sinews, while yet he was an embryo in his mother's womb, and planning his life before he was born. And, as he meditates on the numberless evidences of an all-wise Mind at the heart of things, he falls asleep lost in wonder at God's wisdom, only on waking to find himself still in God's presence. 'When I awake', he says, 'I am still with thee.'

III

Had the psalm ended there, it had been flawless. But now, suddenly, at verse 19, the praising of God gives place to the cursing of men:

> O that thou wouldst slay the wicked, O God, ...
> Men who maliciously defy thee ...
> Do not I hate them that hate thee, O Lord?
> I hate them with a perfect hatred.

For many people, the psalm is marred by this little 'hymn of hate'. They would fain erase it from holy writ. Yet there it stands to serve us for an awful warning.

Our psalmist cannot understand why God can tolerate the continued existence of wicked men who defy him. Charles Murray, the Scottish poet, knew that frame of mind. 'Gin I were God', said he, 'and saw what a hell men were making of my braw, birling earth, I would send another flood and droon oot the hale hypothek.' Can you lay your hand on your heart and say that you have never felt like this when you have seen godless men wrecking and ruining what you knew to be good and true, and apparently 'getting away with it'?

We forget, as the psalmist forgot, that God's thoughts are not our thoughts; and so we wrongly conclude that those whom we hate God must hate too. This is the sin of religion, the sin of Saul the persecutor, the sin of the sectarian zealot in every age, the sin of fanaticism. But, when we bring it to the test of him who on the cross prayed for his crucifiers, 'Father, forgive them, for they know not what they do', we know that this fanaticism is not God's way, we know that it is sin.

IV

Happily, cursing is not the psalmist's last word. The imprecation has hardly died away upon his lips when he realizes it is unworthy, and that he himself is a sinner standing in need of God's forgiveness:

> Search me, O God, and know my heart,
> Try me, and know my thoughts,
> And see if there be any wicked way in me,
> And lead me in the way everlasting.

Dead now is all desire to flee God; quenched now that ugly flame of fanaticism. Now, all we see is a soul naked before his Maker, and asking only for his grace.

We are all in the psalmist's shoes. His is a prayer we all need to make, if ever we have glimpsed God's holiness and, like the publican in the parable, felt our unworthiness to stand in his presence.

Yet we are far more favoured than the psalmist, who belongs to the company of those who 'received not the promise, God having provided some better thing concerning us, that apart from us they should not be made perfect' (Heb. 11.39f.). Since the psalmist wrote, the supreme revelation of God in history has taken place, and we stand in its blessed light. We stand not where the psalmist stood but where Paul stood on the day of his conversion. What staggered Paul on the Damascus Road was not the miracle of a dead prophet's resuscitation. It was that the redemption for which men had long hoped and prayed had now come and was already at work. By Christ's cross and resurrection God had in principle redeemed our race from its sin, and what was now to do was to bring all men to that saving knowledge.

We Christians know, or ought to know, as the psalmist did not, that this besetting God is a holy Father who so loved the world that he gave his only Son for its saving. We Christians know that we cannot flee from God's Spirit, because 'God's love has been poured into our hearts through the Holy Spirit which has been given to us' (Rom. 5.5). We believe that on the cross the decisive battle between good and evil has been fought and won and, that, though the campaign still drags on, God's final triumph over all evil is assured.

'Whither shall I go from thy presence?' asked the psalmist. The answer is: 'Nowhere.' For God is 'now here' – here in Christ incarnate, crucified, risen and regnant; and his last word to us in Christ is: 'See I have redeemed you, and lo, I am with you alway, even unto the end of the world.'

4

The Servant of the Lord

(Isaiah 53)

Were a vote taken among Christians to decide the greatest chapter in the Old Testament, many would choose the 53rd of Isaiah. Here, if anywhere, they would say, is St Augustine's saying true: 'The New Testament lies hidden in the Old, the Old is made plain in the New.'

Isaiah 53 (or, more precisely, Isaiah 52.13–53.12) is the last and greatest of four songs[1] about the Servant of the Lord in the prophecies of Second Isaiah. What Servant of the Lord had the prophet in mind? The nation Israel? A faithful remnant in Israel? Or some individual like Jeremiah? Probably the best answer is that he was depicting a future Saviour-figure who should fulfil all that God meant Israel to be.

I

The Song of the Suffering Servant, consisting of five stanzas, contains the words of both God and men.

First, God declares that his Servant shall succeed: though suffering be his fate, it will lead to undreamt-of vindication:

> Behold, my Servant shall prosper,
>   he shall be exalted and lifted up,
>   and shall be very high.
> As many were astonished at him –
>   his appearance was so marred, beyond human semblance,
>   and his form beyond that of the sons of men –
> so shall he startle many nations;
>   kings shall shut their mouths because of him;
> for that which has not been told them they shall see,
>   and that which they have not heard they shall understand
>   (52.13-15).

Whereupon the people exclaim: 'This is incredible! There was nothing in the Servant's appearance to attract us; when he suffered, we supposed God was punishing him. But, blind though we were (they continue), we now see that it was by God's will that he was suffering for *our* sins:

> Who has believed what we have heard?
>> and to whom has the arm of the Lord been revealed?
> For he grew up before him like a young plant,
>> and like a root out of dry ground;
> he had no form or comeliness that we should look at him,
>> and no beauty that we should desire him.
> He was despised and rejected by men;
>> a man of sorrows and acquainted with grief;
> and as one from whom men hide their faces
>> he was despised, and we esteemed him not.
> Surely he has borne our griefs
>> and carried our sorrows;
> yet we esteemed him stricken,
>> smitten by God and afflicted.
> But he was wounded for our transgressions,
>> he was bruised for our iniquities;
> upon him was the chastisement that made us whole,
>> and with his stripes we are healed.
> All we like sheep have gone astray;
>> we have turned every one to his own way;
> and the Lord has laid on him
>> the iniquity of us all'   (53.1-6).

In the final two stanzas God, through his prophet, tells how the Servant was led like a lamb to the slaughter and, though innocent, done to ignominious death. But (ends the song) all this was part of God's purpose. The Servant who poured out his life for sinners shall yet be vindicated, see the light[2] of God's salvation, and thereby become the saviour of many.

> He was oppressed, and he was afflicted,
>> Yet he opened not his mouth;
> Like a lamb that is led to the slaughter,
>> and like a sheep that before its shearers is dumb,
>> so he opened not his mouth.
> By oppression and judgment he was taken away;
>> and as for his generation, who considered
>> that he was cut off out of the land of the living,

stricken for the transgression of my people?
And they made his grave with the wicked
    and with a rich man in his death,
although he had done no violence,
    and there was no deceit in his mouth.
Yet it was the will of the Lord to bruise him;
    he has put him to grief;
when he makes himself an offering for sin,
    he shall see his offspring, he shall prolong his days;
the will of the Lord shall prosper in his hand;
    he shall see the fruit of the travail of his soul and
        be satisfied;
by his knowledge shall the righteous one, my servant,
    make many to be accounted righteous;
    and he shall bear their iniquities.
Therefore I will divide him a portion with the great,
    and he shall divide the spoil with the strong;
because he poured out his soul to death,
    and was numbered with the transgressors;
yet he bore the sin of many,
    and made intercession for the transgressors (53.7-12).

As we read these words, some of us think of the early Christian hymn, quoted by Paul in Philippians 2.6-11, which sings the praise of one who 'taking the form of a servant' became 'obedient even unto death', and whom God 'highly exalted', giving him 'the name above every name'.

And all down the centuries since, Christians have found in Isaiah's song a foreshadowing of the Church's Lord. Its Fulfiller, they have claimed, is Jesus the Son of Mary and of God, who knew himself to be God's Servant Messiah, as his words about his passion again and again echo this chapter of Isaiah.[3] George Adam Smith in his commentary on Isaiah[4] wrote:

> The most striking thing about this prophecy is the spectral appearance of the Servant ... We hear of him, but he does not speak. We see faces he startles, lips that the sight of him shuts, but himself we see not. Who was he then? Where shall we find him? Has he come?

> About five hundred and fifty years after this prophecy was written, a Man came forward from among the sons of men – among this very nation from whom the prophecy had arisen; and in every essential of consciousness and of experience He was the counterpart, embodiment and fulfilment of this Suffering Servant and his Service. Jesus Christ answers the questions which the prophecy

raises and leaves unanswered. In the prophecy we see one who is only a spectre, a dream, a conscience without a voice, without a name, without a place in history. But in Jesus Christ the dream becomes a reality.

II

Only after the Holy Spirit's coming did Christ's followers begin to see that the cross accorded with God's purpose in Isaiah 53. But see it they did; for the first article in the very early statement of Christian belief in I Corinthians 15.3ff. affirms that 'Christ died for our sins according to the scriptures.' True, the scriptures are not specified; but as Wheeler Robinson once said to the present writer, 'If Paul had added an explanatory footnote here, it would have been: "See Isaiah 53".'

The first explicit application of the chapter to Jesus in the New Testament comes in the story of Philip the evangelist and the Ethiopian (Acts 8.26-40).

The scene is a desert road leading down from Jerusalem to Gaza, the last town in Palestine on the way to Egypt. Philip, fresh from his missionary success in Samaria, is trudging southwards when the coach of the Ethiopian queen's treasurer draws abreast, and to his surprise Philip hears him reading aloud from a scroll (as the rabbis said the law should be read on a journey). There can be no mistaking the chapter he is studying; it is Isaiah 53. So Philip is moved to ask, 'Do you understand what you are reading?' 'How can I', answers the African, 'without someone to guide me? If you can help me, come up into my carriage.'

The mysterious words concern that Servant of the Lord who was led like a lamb to the slaughter and by whose hurt the many may be healed. 'Of whom is the prophet talking, of himself, or of someone else?' 'Not of himself', answers Philip, 'but of another.' Then, identifying that other, Philip tells the African 'the good news of Jesus' – tells him of that supreme vicarious Sufferer in whose ministry, death, resurrection and exaltation Isaiah's prophecy had been fulfilled.

III

Philip however was not the first to apply Isaiah 53 to the church's Lord and find in it the solution to the 'scandal' of the cross. Who then was? The New Testament evidence points to the man on whom Jesus had said he would build his church (Matt. 16.18).[5]

Four times in Acts 3 and 4 Jesus is called 'God's Servant' (*pais tou theou*). Twice this title occurs on Peter's own lips (Acts 3.13, 26), and twice in prayer where Peter is present (Acts 4.27, 30). Does it not sound as if 'God's Servant' – the Servant-Saviour of Isaiah's prophecy – was Peter's preferred title for his crucified and risen Master?

At Caesarea Philippi (Mark 8.32ff.), so little understanding of a suffering Messiah had Peter shown that he drew down on himself his Master's sharp rebuke, 'Your Messiah is a conqueror; God's Messiah is a servant!' Then we recall that, according to the earliest Christian 'tradition' we possess, (I Cor. 15.3ff.), the risen Christ 'appeared first to Cephas' (which is Peter's nickname in Aramaic). Is it not consonant with all we know about the volatile Peter that, after the Easter victory, he should have made the great *volte face* and been the first to proclaim what previously he had thought incredible – the necessity of Jesus' dying as God's Servant in order to reign and redeem?

As if to confirm this, in the second chapter of Peter's first epistle, we find him boldly and fully applying Isaiah 53 to Christ (I Peter 2.21-25).

One last stone upon the cairn of proof. According to Papias, the early church father, Mark's gospel is the record of Jesus' work and words written when he, John Mark, 'acted as Peter's interpreter'. Now Mark's gospel contains many sayings of Jesus which echo Isaiah 53 (above all, the 'ransom saying' of Mark 10.45), as it ends with 'the young man' by the empty grave repeating Jesus' message to the women, 'Go and tell my disciples *and Peter*' (Mark 16.7). Are we not warranted in here detecting Peter's own emphasis and testimony? The man who had tried hardest to divert Jesus from the way of the cross was the first after the resurrection to proclaim that the suffering and victory of Jesus, God's Servant Son, had been according to his Father's will and purpose declared in prophecy?

Notes

1. The other Servant Songs are: Isaiah 42.1-4; 49.1-6; 50.4-9.

2. In Isaiah 53.11, instead of the AV 'shall see of the travail of his soul', the NEB (on the same lines as the Jerusalem Bible), with good warrant from the Septuagint and the Dead Sea Scroll of Isaiah, reads: 'After all his pains he shall be bathed in light.' So Paul saw the risen Lord on the Damascus road.

3. For an impressive proof of this, see J. Jeremias, *The Servant of God*, rev. ed., SCM Press and Allenson 1965, pp. 80-106.

4. George Adam Smith, *The Book of Isaiah*, vol. 2, rev. ed., Hodder & Stoughton and Doubleday, Doran & Co. 1927, pp. 381f.

5. See O. Cullmann, *The Christology of the New Testament*, 2nd ed., SCM Press and Westminster Press 1963, pp. 73ff.

5

Jesus Ben Sira

The adjective 'apocryphal' commonly describes something of doubt-ful truth. No such stigma necessarily attaches to the Greek noun from which it comes. The Apocrypha (lit. 'hidden things') are the fifteen books in the Greek and Latin translations of the Old Testament (known as the Septuagint and the Vulgate) which do not appear in the Old Testament canon accepted by Jews and many Protestants.

By common consent the gem among these books is Ecclesiasticus, or, 'the Wisdom of Jesus Ben Sira'. In *The Oxford Dictionary of Quotations* no less than twenty-eight of its forty citations from the Apocrypha are drawn from it. And Ecclesiasticus, which means 'the Church Book', so far from figuring on any *Index Expurgatorius*, has long been read with profit by both Jews and Christians, and highly esteemed alike for its wisdom and its wit. In 1970 it was freshly and finely translated in *The New English Bible* (from which most of our quotations will be taken).

Where and when was the book written?

It was Jerusalem, and in Hebrew, that Ben Sira wrote his book nearly two hundred years before the birth of Christ, who may well have known it.[1] About 132 BC, Ben Sira's grandson, who had settled in Egypt, turned it into Greek, the *lingua franca* of the time. And ever since we suspect there have been many who would gladly have seen 'the Church Book' in the Old Testament canon in place of the canonical but lugubrious Ecclesiastes, whose name means 'the Preacher', though of good news he has little.

I

'All wisdom is from the Lord', Ben Sira begins (after a graceful preface by his grandson), and indeed his dominant theme is 'wis-dom'. For him, this word comprises all sorts of aptitudes and activities – clever craftsmanship and business acumen, sound learning and self-discipline, shrewd dealing and right living. All these good gifts, he says, come from above. The all-wise God gives some of this wisdom to all men, and a great deal to those who love him. 'If', says Ben Sira, 'you discover a wise man, rise early to visit him, and let your feet wear out his doorstep' (6.36).

For 'old Ben' (as we may affectionately name him) there is only one right way to live a wise life, namely, in accordance with the divine commandments contained in the law (or torah); for 'the fear of the Lord', that is, reverence for God and his revealed will, is the beginning of all man's wisdom.

Accordingly, in his fifty-one chapters we find a close connexion between divine Wisdom and everyday life, as he discusses such themes as man's life under God's providence, religion in the home, social behaviour, the use and abuse of money, the splendours of God's world, and the heroes in Israel's roll of honour.

Beyond doubt best known of all his chapters is the 44th, beginning, 'Let us now praise famous men', and containing those words which now stand on many of our war memorials:

> Their bodies were buried in peace;
> but their name liveth for evermore.

Not so well known but hardly less magnificent is his hymn of creation in chapter 43:

> What a masterpiece is the clear vault of the sky!
> How glorious is the spectacle of the heavens!
> The sun comes into view proclaiming as it rises
> how marvellous a thing it is, made by the Most High.
>
> Look at the rainbow and praise its Maker;
> it shines with a supreme beauty,
> rounding the sky with its gleaming arc,
> a bow bent by the hands of the Most High   (43.1f., 11f.).

Here also let us mention two passages in chapter 38, the first on the value of the good physician who, because 'his skill comes from the Most High', prays before he diagnoses; the second, on our debt to those honest men of their hands – ploughmen and potters, craftsmen and smiths – who

> maintain the fabric of this world
> And their prayers are about their daily work   (31.34).

If 'old Ben' is often disconnectedly discursive, he has the gift of style – right words in right places. Epigrams are his stock-in-trade; antithesis his *forte*; he is master of the telling simile; and when he sings the glories of creation, he can write with the lyric power of a Wordsworth, though without trace of pantheism.

Let us hear him on some of his favourite subjects.

II

In Ben Sira's view a prime necessity of life is 'a home with its decent privacy' (29.21) plus 'pure religion breathing household laws'. In that home the Fifth Commandment should prevail:

> Honour your father with all your heart,
> and do not forget your mother's birth-pangs;
> remember that your parents brought you into the world;
> how can you repay what they have done for you?   (7.27f.)

Listen to him counselling the fathers:

> Have you sons? Discipline them
> and break them in from their earliest years.
> Have you daughters? See that they are chaste,
> and do not be too lenient with them.
> Marry your daughter, and a great load will be off your
>   hands;
> but give her to a sensible husband   (7.23-25).

Concerning wives (with just a hint of male chauvinism):

> There is nothing so bad as a bad wife   (25.19).

> A good wife makes a happy husband;
> she doubles the length of his life   (26.1).

> If she has a kind and gentle tongue,
> then her husband is luckier than most men   (36.23).

III

Which brings us to another of his favourite themes – the danger of a foolish tongue. (Compare James 3.1-12 in the New Testament.) 'A man's tongue', he warns, 'may be his downfall' (5.13). Therefore 'think before you speak':

> Answer a man if you know what to say,
> but if not, hold your tongue   (5.12).

('The worst of speaking without thinking', said James Denney, 'is that you say what you think.') Therefore

> Tell no tales about friend or foe; . . .
> Have you heard a rumour? Let it die with you.
> Never fear, it will not make you burst   (19.8, 10).

Again, on swearing (of the sort all too common today):

> Do not inure your mouth to oaths,
> or make a habit of naming the Holy One   (23.9).

With our proverbial 'sticks and stones may break my bones, but names will never hurt me', old Ben refuses to agree:

> The lash of a whip raises weals,
> but the lash of a tongue breaks bones,
> Many have been killed by the sword,
> but not so many as by the tongue   (28.17f.).

IV

From Boswell's pages we know how Doctor Samuel Johnson valued his friends, and how he counselled men to 'keep their friendships in good repair.' Ben Sira is of the same mind:

> A faithful friend is a secure shelter;
> whoever has found one has found a treasure.
> A faithful friend is beyond price;
> his worth is more than money can buy.
> A faithful friend is an elixir of life,
> found only by those who fear the Lord.
> The man who fears the Lord keeps his friendships in repair,
> for he treats his neighbour as himself   (6.14-17).

'Some are friends in name only,' he moralizes, 'they turn against you when trouble comes', but he goes on:

> Never forget a friend,
> or neglect him when prosperity comes your way   (37.1-6).

V

A good work by which Ben Sira sets great store is that of charity, or almsgiving:

> As water quenches a blazing fire,
> So almsgiving atones for sin   (3.30).

'Give to him who asks', says our Lord in his sermon (Matt. 5.42).
Just so Ben Sira counsels:

> If a man is desperate, do not add to his troubles,
> or keep him waiting for the charity he asks.
> Do not reject the appeal of a man in his distress,
> or turn your back on the poor   (4.3f.).

But on the contrary:

> Store up for yourself the treasure which the Most High
>   has commanded,
> and it will benefit you more than gold.
> Let almsgiving be the treasure in your strong-room,
> and it will rescue you from every misfortune   (29.11f.).

And then he gives his reason:

> The rush that grows on every river-bank
> is pulled up before any other grass.
> But kindness is like a luxuriant garden,
> and almsgiving lasts for ever   (40.16).

VI

For Ben Sira, the life of the epicure or the hedonist holds no attraction. 'Gluttony', he declares, 'has been the death of many' (37.31). In moderation, wine is good; but

> Do not try to prove your manhood by drinking,
> for wine has been the ruin of many   (31.25).

What about riches? Wealth is good, if sin has not tainted it (13.24); but 'a passion for gold can never be right' (31.5). 'Health and fitness are better than any gold' (30.15).

No Puritan, Ben Sira is far from banning 'innocent enjoyment' or what we nowadays call 'socializing'. But he insists on decorum and good manners:

> If you are sitting at a grand table,
> do not lick your lips and exclaim, 'What a spread!' . . .
> Eat what is set before you like a gentleman; . . .
> Leave in good time, and do not be the last to go;
> go straight home without lingering ' (31.12, 16; 32.11).

VII

Much of his wisdom is of the prudential and practical kind – that sanctified common-sense which Dr Thomas Chalmers liked to call 'gumption-rummel gumption':

> Do not lend to a man with more influence than yourself,
> or, if you do, write off the loan as a loss   (8.12).

> Do not find fault before examining the evidence;
> think first, and criticize afterwards   (11.7).

or this, which might fit a modern motorist:

> Do not be careless on a clear road
> but watch where you are going   (32.21).

Very realistic he can be about business and banking:

> If your wife is untrustworthy, or where many hands are at
>   work,
> it is well to keep things under lock and key.
> When you make a deposit, see that it is weighed and counted,
> and when you give or receive it, have it all in writing
>
> (42.6ff.).

Cleverness is an advantage, but much to be preferred is goodness:

> Better to be godfearing and lack brains
> Than to have great intelligence and break the law   (19.24).

VIII

So we come back to where we began, to the human wisdom which is a gift of the divine Wisdom. And how easily Ben Sira moves from the one to the other! Thus, having warned against some dubious advisers:

> Never consult a woman about her rival,
> or a coward about war,

he counsels,

> Trust your own judgment, . . .
> But above all, pray to the Most High
> to keep you on the straight road of truth   (37.11-15).

Like Job and St Paul, Ben Sira knows that the human mind cannot fathom the greatness of God:

Has anyone ever seen him, to be able to describe him?
Can anyone praise him as he truly is?
We have seen but a small part of his works,
and there remain many mysteries greater still (43.31ff.).

Yet he remains assured that 'As is his majesty, so also is his mercy' (2.18).

The man who can so speak of God, address him as 'Lord, Father and Ruler of my life' (23.1), and counsel his readers,

Forgive your neighbour his wrongdoing,
then, when you pray, your sins will be forgiven (28.2),

is, like the scribe in the gospels, 'not far from the kingdom of God' (Mark 12.34).

Wise and witty, shrewd and godfearing, such a man is Ben Sira, who bore the human name of our Lord himself. What a wholesome book he has bequeathed to us! How much he says that is still valid today, and how splendidly he says it! Do not, dear reader, let that other 'Preacher', even if he stands in the canon, depress you with his 'vanity of vanities'. As a cordial for drooping spirits, turn rather to the 'Church Book', though doubtfully canonical, and peruse it, both for everyday living and for your spiritual health.

Note

1. Christ's great invitation (Matt. 11.28ff.) seems to echo Ecclus. 51.23, 26f.

PART TWO

THE GOSPEL THEN AND NOW

6

The Beginning of the Gospel

The gospel is the good news of the new face put on life some two thousand years ago when God gave mankind Jesus Christ. Whatever the scholars and critics have made of him, ever since then this Man has meant to millions, as A. J. Gossip once put it, 'a life lived out, a dream of God come true, God's Amen to men', and for this 'inexpressible gift' [as Paul called it] they have given him thanks.

Born in Bethlehem during the reign of the Emperor Augustus, while the *pax Romana* girdled the world, he had grown up in Nazareth of Galilee where he learned the trade of carpenter. When Augustus died in AD 14, he was about twenty years old. Doubtless the news of the great Emperor's death troubled many of his contemporaries, who feared it might mean the end of the Augustan peace and an ordered empire. But Jesus was thinking of another peace and another empire and biding his time.

When, a dozen or more years later, there appeared in the Judaean wilderness (not far from where the Dead Sea Scrolls were found) a prophet named John the Baptist, announcing that the day of the Lord was nigh, Jesus knew that his time had come. From Nazareth he went down to the river Jordan to be baptized by John, and not long after began a ministry in which he would proclaim a kingdom mightier than the Roman – a kingdom in which the King was a heavenly Father and he himself that Father's Son sent for men's saving . . .

I

We have four written gospels narrating the work and words of Jesus the Christ, that is, the Messiah. Among them, the earliest is that compiled by John Mark, a native of Jerusalem (where his mother's home was a rendezvous for the first Christians) and the junior colleague of Christ's two leading apostles, Peter and Paul. Appearing in Rome about AD 65, it was to be followed in the next generation by three others bearing the names of Matthew, Luke and John.

Each evangelist has his own approach to the gospel. St John opens majestically, 'In the beginning was the Word', locating all he is about to tell in the eternal purpose of God. St Matthew and St Luke start with a baby born in Bethlehem; and when they relate the 'virginal conception' by the action of the Holy Spirit, it is their way of saying that God was here uniquely at work, that Jesus was in fact God's Son. By contrast, St Mark begins roughly midway through the reign of Augustus's successor, Tiberius, with Jesus' baptism by John in the Jordan.

Diverse beginnings, then, but all four evangelists go on to tell the same basic story, traditionally known as 'the ministry of Jesus'. The word 'ministry' fitly describes the work of One who knew himself called to be a Messiah, or Saviour, after the pattern of Isaiah's Servant of the Lord, and to inaugurate the kingdom of God his Father among men.

Let us be clear however what this key-phrase[1] in the gospels really means. Our concept of its nature and coming has often been all too human and static. We have thought of the kingdom of God as a spiritual commonwealth embracing all who do God's will, or perhaps as a Christian socialist paradise to be set up on earth by the hands of men. But in the New Testament the kingdom of God means the kingly rule of God, and it is nothing if not *dynamic*. It is *God's sovereign power becoming manifestly effective* in the world of human experience, as for centuries devout Jews had prayed and hoped it would. It is the living God, from the invisible beyond, invading history in order to deliver men from their sins and sorrows, and the new order of things thus established.

Now it was the very heart of Jesus' good news that this supreme event – this blessed time – was no longer a shining hope on the far horizon but a dawning reality. 'The time has come', he cried, 'the kingdom of God is upon you: repent and believe the Gospel' (Mark 1.15 NEB; cf. Isa. 52.7-10).

At last, and in accordance with prophecy, God was visiting his people in grace and judgment, and doing so in his own work and words. 'If I by the finger of God cast out devils', he said, 'then the kingdom of God has come upon you.' (Luke 11.20)

Dynamic likewise must be our concept of the ministry in which God's kingdom took effect. Too often we have pictured its first phase

28

as a quiet pastoral idyll –

> O sabbath rest by Galilee,
> O calm of hills above

– in contrast with the later stormy period in Judaea, culminating in Jesus' 'passion'. A distinction there was in outward setting, but not in purpose. From Galilee to Golgotha it was one long campaign in which Jesus strove mightily against the powers of evil which hold men's lives in thrall.

Again, we have been wont to think of Jesus' parables as picturesque moralizing tales, when many of them were in fact 'weapons of war' in his verbal cut-and-thrust with the scribes and Pharisees, as in answer to those censorious men he brought the grace of God to outcasts whom they deemed beyond its pale. Or, perhaps in deference to modern man's scepticism about them, we have 'played down' Jesus' miracles, not perceiving that they were mostly outgoings in power of that love which was central to the kingdom of God. Above all, we have sometimes missed seeing that Jesus, who chose to be known as 'the Son of man'[2], not only announced the kingdom's dawning but himself embodied it – was the kingdom incarnate – as his divine warfare against sin, disease and death found its climax in a deed 'determined, dared and done', by his Father's appointing, on a cross.

Jesus Christ, then, was not merely, as some would have it, a sublime teacher come to give mankind the sermon on the mount and the story of the Prodigal Son, though for both the world is deeply in his debt. He was the strong and compassionate Son of God come to set the earth aflame with the heavenly fire (Luke 12.49f.) and 'destroy the works of the devil' (I John 3.8).

II

Now, basing ourselves on Mark's gospel, but drawing also on the other three, not least St John's which, besides offering the profoundest interpretation, preserves much valuable historical tradition,[3] let us outline the ministry of Jesus.

We begin at Jordan with John the Baptist. This grim, great man, 'a prophet and more than a prophet' (Luke 7.26), believing the day of judgment to be near, called on his countrymen to repent and be baptized for the forgiveness of their sins.

Among those who submitted to his baptism – thus even then 'numbering himself with the transgressors' (Isa. 53.12) – was Jesus. As he rose streaming from Jordan, the tale of that traffic between two worlds, which holds the key to his whole ministry, began with a transcendent experience in which he was confirmed as God's Servant Son and the Bearer of God's saving rule to men, i.e. the Messiah (Mark 1.9-11).

When the news reached him that Herod Antipas had put John the Baptist in prison, Jesus came into Galilee announcing the dawning of God's kingdom and calling on his hearers to 'turn back' to God and make the good news their own. With an authority which astounded the worshippers he taught in the synagogues, while in towns like Capernaum, Chorazin and Bethsaida he went about healing the sick and the spiritually deranged, so that his fame ran through Galilee and beyond it.

But his consorting with outcasts and sinners, his 'cavalier' attitude to the law of Moses and the sabbath, and his claim to be the divine pardon incarnate, so shocked the Jewish churchmen that, in order to prosecute his ministry, he had to quit the synagogues for the lakeside. There he continued to spearhead God's warfare against the powers of evil, by his 'mighty works' manifesting the kingdom's presence, and in his parables challenging men to decision for or against it.

Twelve men whom he had chosen and trained to be the nucleus of the new Israel, or people of God, he now dispatched to announce God's dawning kingdom by word and deed. Such was the excitement following their return from mission that thousands thronged after Jesus to the north end of the lake. There, in a desert place, he fed them with the bread of the kingdom or, as St John calls it, 'the bread of life' (Mark 6.30-44; John 6.1-40). It was the Galilean Lord's Supper. Jesus had come 'not to invite the righteous but sinners' (Mark 2.17) to the banquet of God's kingdom; and there he was now doing it, acting out his own parable of the Great Supper (Luke 14.15-24), in hope that the men of Galilee would align themselves with God's high purpose incarnate in himself.

Alas, by their reaction (John 6.15), they betrayed how earth-bound were their notions of God's kingdom. What they were dreaming of was 'a revolt in the desert' against hated Rome, with Jesus cast in the role of leader. Long before, in the wilderness (Matt. 4.8-10), Jesus had rejected this sort of Messiahship as a very temptation of the devil. So now, for a time, with the twelve he withdrew out of Galilee, away from the dangerous enthusiasm of his followers, that in quiet communion with his Father he might learn his will.

By the time they had reached Caesarea Philippi, in the shadow of Mount Hermon, it had been revealed to him. Messiah he was, as Peter now confessed him to be, but a Messiah who must go to his throne by way of a gibbet (Mark 8.27-33). When Peter protested 'Never!', Jesus turned on him saying, 'You think as man thinks, not as God thinks.' If God's reign were to come 'with power', he said, a *via dolorosa* stretched out before him and his (Mark 8.34-9.1). The time had come when he must carry God's offensive into the very heart and home of Jewry.

The transfiguration, six days later, on a mountain-top (Mark 9.2-6; Luke 9.28-36) was the counterpart in the disciples' experience of the baptism in Jesus' own. In vision something of their Master's true stature and destiny was disclosed to Peter, James and John. Then began the journey southward, through Galilee, to Jerusalem.

Followed a ministry of some three months in Jerusalem, from the feast of Tabernacles to that of Dedication (John 7.10; 10.22), in which Jesus challenged the rulers of Israel with the crisis of divine judgment now overhanging them, and in parables urged the people to repent before the darkness overtook them and the door of the kingdom was shut against them (John 12.35f.; Matt. 25.1-13). The response was, first, an attempt to arrest him and, later, a threat to stone him (John 7.32-52; 10.31). That crisis Jesus now met, as he had met the earlier one in Galilee, by withdrawing – this time across the Jordan to where the Baptist had once baptized (John 10.40). There, in Trans-Jordan, his purpose crystallized in the decision to return to Jerusalem at the approaching Passover (John 11.55ff.: April, AD 30) and finish his God-given work (John 4.34; 19.30).

Now ensued the events we associate with Holy Week: the entry into Jerusalem 'in lowly pomp', the cleansing of the temple, the priests' plot, the defection of Judas, the Last Supper, the arrest, trial and condemnation, the crucifixion, death and burial, all recounted with stark realism in Mark 14.1-15.47. On the evening of the first Good Friday Jesus lay dead in his rock-tomb; his disciples had gone into hiding; the curtain seemed to have fallen on unrelieved human tragedy . . .

Man proposes, but God disposes. That seeming tragedy God turned into triumph. On the first Easter morning three women found his tomb empty; the risen Christ came back in glory to his own, commissioning them as his apostles. The Christian era had begun, its first fruits the infant church, soon, at Pentecost, to be invested with 'power from on high' for its mission to the wider world.

Notes

1. The phrase occurs 85 times in the gospels. St Matthew prefers the

phrase 'the kingdom of heaven'; but the meaning is the same, the words 'of heaven' illustrating the pious Jew's avoidance of the name of God.

2. In Daniel 7, the probable source of the title, 'one like a son of man' is the Head of the new people of God destined to receive 'dominion and glory and a kingdom'.

3. See C. H. Dodd, *Historical Tradition in the Fourth Gospel*, Cambridge University Press 1963.

7

The Cross

So I saw in my dream that, as Christian came up with the cross, his burden loosed from off his back, and began to tumble, and so continued to do, till it came to the mouth of the sepulchre, where it fell in, and I saw it no more. Then was Christian glad and lightsome, and said with a merry heart, 'He hath given me rest by his sorrow, and life by his death.'

So we read in Bunyan's great allegory, *The Pilgrim's Progress*. Christian of course is Bunyan himself; and, though many of us do not come to Christ in quite the way he did, his words find an answering echo in our hearts. The cross, we perceive, is the diamond pivot on which the story of our redemption turns, the means whereby we are healed of our soul's sore hurt.

But how did that strange man on his cross become 'the Saviour of the world'?

I

Recall our Lord's ministry. Authenticated as God's Son at his baptism, Jesus knew himself called to be the Messiah who must walk the way appointed for the Servant of the Lord in Isaiah. From the very outset, then, he must have reckoned with the possibility of a tragic *dénouement* to his work. At Caesarea Philippi the possibility had become a certainty. The Son of man, he told the twelve, *must* suffer and be killed (Mark 8.31). For him death was now a necessity if his Father's kingdom were to be effectuated 'in power' (Mark 9.1). We may surmise that this terrible truth was revealed to him by his heavenly Father and confirmed by his own study of scripture. At any rate, from now on, most of his sayings about his approaching death have the sombre music of Isaiah 53 somewhere in the background.

Jesus, to be sure, did not come to preach the atonement but that there might be an atonement to preach. None the less, on his way to Calvary, he gave his disciples hint after vivid hint of the necessity and purpose of his dying. It was a *cup* of suffering his Father had given him to drink, in order to initiate a new covenant, or order of relations, between God and men (Mark 10.38; 14.23f.). It was a *baptism* in blood whereby many would be cleansed from the defilement of their sins (Mark 10.38; Luke 12.49). It was a *road* to be travelled, a road marked out in scripture which ended in death (Mark 14.21). It was a *ransom* which, as the Lord's Servant, he must pay, if 'the many' (which is Hebrew for 'all') were to be delivered from the doom which overhung them (Mark 10.45). Thus, by one metaphor after another, Jesus signalled at the meaning of his God-given work ere it was done.

In the literal sense of the word Jesus' death was not a sacrifice but a miscarriage of justice brought about by Jew and Roman acting in their own self-interest. But, as John Ruskin said, 'The great mystery of the idea of sacrifice itself is that you cannot save men from death but by facing it for them, nor from sin but by resisting it.' In this sense Jesus' death was a sacrifice. It was his willingness to accept what others forced on him and to see it as a sacrifice which he could offer to God that transformed an act of human sin into an act of divine redemption. In the cross we find the supreme illustration of Joseph's words to his brothers: 'As for you, you meant evil against me; but God meant it for good, to bring it about that many people should be kept alive' (Gen. 50.20). There, at Calvary, God in Christ so died that sin lost its chief servant, death, which henceforth, by God's gracious appointing, became the minister of life – eternal life – for 'many people'. Thus we may see how man proposes but God disposes, how things willed by sinful men are yet worked upon by God and, by a stroke of divine irony, man's greatest crime turns into God's greatest blessing.

Here it is worth observing that, if the disciples' last glimpse of their Master had been of him hanging on the cross, these passion sayings of his which we have mentioned would never have been remembered, nor possibly would Jesus himself. It was the resurrection and the coming of the Spirit which taught his followers to see the cross not as stark tragedy brought about by men who 'knew not what they did' but as the divine way of making sinners 'one with the goodness of God himself' (II Cor. 5.21, NEB).

II

Half a dozen years later (as I Cor. 15.3ff. shows) the apostles had reached a common finding about the meaning of the cross: 'Christ died for our sins according to the scriptures.' Chief among those scriptures must have been Isaiah 53, which tells of God's suffering Servant who 'bore the sin of many'.

Yet each of the apostolic writers saw the cross from his own particular angle.

When, in Acts 3 and 4 and in his first letter, we find Peter identifying his risen Lord with 'God's Servant', we perceive that he has now grasped the truth from which at Caesarea Philippi he had once recoiled in horror.

Among the apostles, however, it was not Peter the rough fisherman but Paul the trained theological thinker who penetrated most deeply into the mystery of the cross. Once (Rom. 3.25) he says that Christ crucified has become for all men what the 'mercy seat' (*hilasterion*; see Ex. 25.15-22) symbolized for old Israel – the place where God draws near and shows his mercy for sinners. Yet perhaps his profoundest word on the cross comes in II Corinthians 5.21 where, explaining how God 'made Christ sin' for our sakes, he depicts the cross as a deed wherein, by God's appointing, our condemnation came upon the sinless Christ that for us there might be condemnation no more.

For St John, Christ is 'the lamb of God who takes away the world's sin'. He 'dies to make men holy' (cf. John 17.19), so that by his sacrifice men may be cleansed from sin (I John 1.7) and foretaste eternal life here and now.

In Hebrews, Christ is portrayed as our great and merciful High Priest who, by the offering up of his own sinless life in obedience to God's will, had opened up for us 'a new and living way' into the holy of holies, which is heaven (Heb. 10.1-22).

Thus, through the New Testament there runs one mighty thought: Christ died for our sins, bore what we should have borne, did for us what was God's good pleasure, did for us what we could never have done for ourselves.

III

Down succeeding centuries the best minds of the church have sought to interpret the cross to their contemporaries in ways they could understand.

All have agreed with John and Paul that *the cross reveals the love of God for sinners* (John 3.16; 1 John 4.10; Rom. 5.8). Yet, if we take this to be the whole truth, we come short of the mind of Christ who knew himself called not simply to *reveal* God's love, but, as God's Representative, to *do* something for men which they could never have done for themselves.

So, second, most Christian thinkers have gone further and, with the apostles, agreed that *Christ bore our sins*. But how? By so identifying himself with our prodigal human race that he entered with us, and for us, into the divine judgment that must ever rest upon human sin. The 'cup' Christ had to drink was 'the cup our sins had mingled', and in the agony of Gethsemane and the dereliction of the cross he is to be seen drinking it to the bitter dregs.

No one may claim to have fathomed the whole mystery of the cross, for

> None of the ransomed ever knew
> How deep were the waters crossed.

Yet perhaps none has come nearer than the saintly John McLeod Campbell in his *The Nature of the Atonement*. Christ, he said, as our Representative, offered on the cross a perfect confession of our sins, a confession which could be described as 'a perfect Amen in humanity to the judgment of God on the sin of man'.[1] To the divine wrath against our sin he responded, 'Righteous art Thou, O Lord, who judgest so.' And by that perfect response he absorbed it, so making possible our forgiveness by holy God.

If any should find that this doctrine outgoes his comprehension, let us put its truth in a homely parable.

You and I are like the boy who has misbehaved and been sent to his room in disgrace. There he sits, sullen and resentful. Suddenly he becomes aware of the presence of his elder brother in the room. 'Surely he hasn't done wrong?' be muses. Then on his elder brother's face he sees a look which he cannot quite fathom. It almost looks as if he were glad to be there. Thereupon the elder brother says: 'All is forgiven. Father will take you back, for my sake. Come with me.' So, shamefacedly, the boy goes. But as he enters his father's presence, he catches the same look on his face as he had seen on his elder brother's. And the father takes him into his arms and forgives him.

Such is the Saviour's work *for* us. Thus we are 'accepted in the beloved' (Eph. 1.6, AV). Yet, to be effective, it must also be Christ's work *in* us. And this it becomes when we put our trust, for time and for eternity, in our crucified and living Lord, when round the sacramental table we partake of 'Christ's love tokens to his body the church', and when, in our everyday living, we seek to serve our fellow-men in love for the sake of him who first loved us and died and rose for our salvation.

Note

1. John McLeod Campbell, *The Nature of the Atonement*, Macmillan 1856, p. 134.

36

8

The Resurrection

By the truth or falsity of the resurrection Christianity stands or falls. If the story of Jesus ends at the cross, not only is our 'good news' a lie and our faith an empty husk (I Cor. 15.21), but it is unmitigated tragedy and – what is more – the supreme proof of the irrationality of the universe in which we live. If the resurrection is true, why then –

> Easter Day breaks!
> Christ rises! Mercy every way
> Is infinite – and who can say?

Consider it then, first as fact, then as experience, and finally as hope.

I

For the fact, the New Testament contains two distinct strands of historical evidence: (*a*) testimony to various appearances of the risen Christ, and (*b*) testimony to the emptiness of the tomb on the first Easter morning. You will find the earliest record of the appearance in I Corinthians 15.1-8, that for the finding of the empty tomb in Mark 16.1-8.

Observe, first, that what may be called the summary of 'things most surely believed' in I Corinthians 15 can be shown to go back, in substance, to within half a dozen years of the crucifixion – is in fact the oldest piece of Christian tradition we possess. (Paul probably got it on his first visit to Jerusalem – see Gal. 1.18f. – after his conversion.) It records six appearances of the risen Christ: three to individuals (Peter, James the Lord's brother, and Paul), and three to groups of people (the twelve, 'more than five hundred brethren' and 'all the apostles'). This is *early* evidence indeed. But, equally important, it is evidence which was *open to testing*; for when Paul wrote to the Corinthians in AD 55, Peter and James were still alive, and so were most of those 'five hundred brethren'. Here then is testimony which passes every reasonable test of historical reliability. Doubt it, and you might as well doubt everything else in the New Testament.

Alongside it we have to set the evidence in Mark 16.1-8 for the empty tomb. This too, though we cannot date it so precisely as I Corinthians 15.1-8, is also early. (Scholars tell us that the story of Christ's passion was the first piece of gospel tradition to be set down in a connected form, with a narrative of the discovery of the empty tomb like that in Mark 16 as its climax, thus making the resurrection God's answer to Christ's cry of dereliction from the cross.) Study Mark 16.1-8 with a good commentary, and you cannot fail to note how sober and self-evidencing it is. A very distinguished modern historian[1] thus concludes his study of the passage: 'If we test what is here capable of being tested, we cannot shake Mark's narrative of the empty tomb.'

What should next be noted is that these two distinct strands of evidence originated independently. The story of the empty tomb does not record an appearance of the risen Christ, and concerns not the disciples but three women. On the other hand, the record of Christ's appearances to his disciples had originally no connexion with the locality of the grave. Thus our two independent strands of evidence complement and confirm each other, showing that belief in the resurrection is rooted not in fantasy but in fact.

Supporting this documentary evidence stand three great witnesses: first, the church of Christ. If the crucifixion had ended the disciples' fellowship with Jesus, it is hard to understand how the church could ever have come into existence, and harder still to understand how it has lasted two thousand years. Second: the New Testament. Every book in the New Testament is a resurrection document in the sense that but for belief in it it would never have been written. Nay, it is not too much to say, with William Manson, that 'the only God the New Testament knows anything about is the God of the Resurrection'.[2] Third: the Lord's Day. No Christian Jew would have changed the sacred day from the Sabbath (Saturday) to 'the first day of the week' except for the reason that on this day he was first seen victorious over death.

If, as David S. Cairns said, the resurrection is the land where the great rivers run, it is also the land where the great mists lie. No mortal eye saw Christ rise; none knows how it happened. Yet, to judge by what the evangelists and St Paul tell us about the form of the risen Christ, they never supposed it to be the story of Lazarus all over again, that is, a dead man resuscitated to his former life and doomed to die again. What they suggest is a Christ who has left the grave incorruptibly, his earthly body having been transformed by God into a heavenly one, from which he manifested himself to the apostles and others.

After the first Easter day the fuller significance of this stupendous miracle – the 'break-in' of the end-time into this world of sin and death – began to dawn on Christ's followers. Nature had echoed and rung to Christ's faith in his heavenly Father. On the work of the cross God had set his shining seal. The living God had vindicated his Son, and in vindicating him, had vindicated his righteousness. And Christ's triumph over 'the last enemy' was, like the breaching of a North Sea dyke, an event of seemingly small importance whose consequences were yet cosmic (see Eph. 1 and Col. 1.). For if one, and he the one who carried in his own person the whole future of God's people, had exploded the myth of death's invincibility, a new creation had begun, bringing with it life – new, divine life for all who were Christ's.

II

Not simply after death but here and now. This is what we mean by the resurrection as an experience – an ongoing experience. Early Christian belief in the resurrection was not confined to those who had seen the risen Christ or visited the gaping tomb. It did not rest solely or simply on other people's report or hearsay, but upon *a corporate spiritual awareness* of the living Christ, no longer as a dead memory, however vivid, but as a vivifying and life-giving presence. They knew themselves to be in fellowship with a living Lord. 'I live, yet not I', said Paul, 'but Christ who lives in me' (Gal. 2.20). 'You have not seen him', Peter tells his readers, 'yet you love him, and are transported with a joy too deep for words' (I Peter 1.8). It was this same living Christ whom John of Patmos heard, through the Holy Spirit, saying to him, 'Fear not, I am the first and the last, and the living one, and behold, I am alive for evermore' (Rev. 1.17f.).

Nor did this sense of Christ as a vivifying presence fade and die as the years passed by. It went on, as it still goes on. Down the centuries there have been countless Christians – from Polycarp of Smyrna to David Livingstone, from Samuel Rutherford of Anwoth to Grenfell of Labrador, from Dale of Birmingham to Bonhoeffer of Hitler's Germany – to testify with one voice, 'Christ is alive! He has had dealings with us, and we with him.'

Nay more, have we not ourselves known men and women in whom this living Christ has been quite evidently at work? For them,

> Death's flood has lost its chill
> Since Jesus crossed the river.

They know that their Saviour lives. Already in this life they are 'risen with Christ' (Col. 3.1), risen above the darkness of doubt, risen above all the pettiness of life, risen above all fear of death or the unknown future.

III

Finally, the resurrection of Christ is a hope – our hope founded upon his triumph over death.

> By God's great mercy we have been born again to a living hope through the resurrection of Jesus Christ from the dead, to an inheritance which is imperishable, undefiled and unfading
>
> (I Peter 1.3f.).

What is the nature of this 'living hope'?

First, everlasting life is *God's gift to us in Christ* – the risen and living Christ. *He* is our immortality.

> Only *one* life has ever won the victory over death, and only one life ever can win it, the kind which was in Christ, which is in Christ, and which he shares with all whom faith makes one with him.[2]

In faith-union with this Christ we become 'nurslings of immortality'. 'I know', says the Christian, 'that my Redeemer lives, and because I am his – one of the sinners for whom he died – I hope, by his grace, to be one day where he now is.'

Second, Christians believe in the resurrection of the *body*, that is, man in the fulness of his personality, not, be it noted, in the resurrection of the *flesh* (see I Cor. 15.50). As God raised his Son from death's sleep, so, in his own good time, he will rouse from their sleep those who are Christ's, and they will make their abode with him in his Father's house (John 14.2).

The New Testament does not promise a blessed life hereafter for all and sundry, regardless of what they have been and done in this life. Rather 'the gospel within the gospels' (John 3.16) envisages the possibility of 'perishing', of some by their inveterate sinning putting themselves beyond the reach even of God's mighty love. What the gospel does affirm is that Christ is a living Lord who promises, 'Because I live, you shall live also' (John 14.19), that by faith and love we may be made one with him as a branch is grafted into the living tree, and that, thus united with him, we too may hope to vanquish 'the last enemy' when, at God's touch, we awake from the sleep of death.

Let this study of the resurrection end as it began, with the paramount importance of the resurrection of Christ for Christian faith.

It is the Easter victory which shows us that God and his love for his wayward children are invincible; for it is at Easter that God, who is under no conceivable obligation to do any such thing, gives back to men the Christ they had rejected, the Christ who died and is now alive for evermore.

Notes

1. H. von Campenhausen, *Tradition and Life in the Church*, Collins and Fortress Press 1968, p. 77. If Mark's account of the finding of the empty tomb is impressive in its sheer sobriety, St John's account of Mary's encounter with the risen Christ in the garden (John 20.10-18) is, of all the appearance stories, perhaps the most veridical. C. H. Dodd wrote that it had 'something indefinably first-hand about it. There is nothing quite like it in the Gospels. Is there anything quite like it in ancient literature?' See 'The Appearances of the Risen Christ: an Essay in Form-criticism of the Gospels' in *Studies in the Gospels*, ed. D. E. Nineham, Blackwell 1955, p. 20.

2. James Denney, *The Way Everlasting*, Hodder & Stoughton and Doran 1911, p. 188.

9

The Holy Spirit

When St Paul reached Ephesus in AD 53, he was shocked to find there about a dozen Christian converts who had never even heard that there was a Holy Spirit (Acts 19.1-6). This grave defect in their Christianity he proceeded at once to remedy. If Paul were to come back today, he might find a not dissimilar situation – many Christians to whom the Third Person of the Trinity means little or nothing, so that their religion has become what Karl Barth called 'flat-tyre' Christianity. The *pneuma*, which is Greek for both 'air' and 'spirit', has gone out of it, and every motorist knows how little progress is to be made when a 'pneumatic' tyre loses its *pneuma*!

How different it was in the church's glad springtime! Come to the letters of the apostles with fresh eyes, and you cannot mistake the tremendous emphasis they put upon the reality of the Holy Spirit. It was, said David S. Cairns,[1] 'like a kind of "wireless" between earth and heaven', turning every Christian congregation into 'a kind of replica of the Galilean circle, with the living Christ still in the midst, messages continually coming and going'. More, as the Acts of the Apostles shows, the Holy Spirit was the divine dynamic which enabled Christ's envoys in less than three decades to carry the good news from Jerusalem to Rome.

I

When we sing in church, 'Breathe on me, Breath of God' or 'I feel the winds of God today', we talk about the Spirit as the Bible does. The Hebrew word for 'spirit' is *ruach*, the Greek *pneuma*. Both signify 'air in motion', be it 'wind' or 'breath'. Something in the physical world – wind ruffling the water's surface or the breath of a living creature – symbolizes that incorporeal element in man we call his 'spirit'.

Then the word is applied to a supernatural power which man feels working in himself and which he believes to come from 'the larger

42

world' – to be divine. The Holy Spirit is the wind or breath of the Almighty, who energizes in creation, works in history, and activates the life of man.

In the Old Testament the Spirit stands chiefly for the *vital energy* of the divine nature, the source at once of abnormal skill, prophetic inspiration, and moral purity. As yet the Spirit of God seems to work fitfully and individually, and later prophets like Ezekiel and Joel look forward to a blessed time when God's Spirit will not only revivify the 'dead bones' of his people but be outpoured on all mankind.

Turn to the New Testament, and you find these prophecies in process of fulfilment, first in the life, death and resurrection of Jesus the Messiah, and then in the church of Christ.

During his ministry Jesus embodies the strong Spirit of God (Matt. 12.28; Luke 10.21; John 14.10). It is the secret of his mighty works and words, the secret too of his unique communion with the one whom he called 'Abba, Father', as of his openness to the needs of suffering and sinful folk. Strengthened by that Spirit, Jesus 'sets his face resolutely towards Jerusalem' and death, and by the same Spirit he is raised from the dead (Rom. 1.4; 8.11).

On their last night together, in the upper room – witness his sayings (John 14-16) concerning the Paraclete, or 'Other Helper' – Jesus, looking beyond the cross, had promised his disciples that the Spirit who had been incarnate in himself, would indwell them also. At Pentecost it all began to happen. The power which had wrought in Jesus – and was now for ever inseparable from him so that they often spoke of 'the Spirit of Jesus' – came upon that motley crowd of individuals, fusing them into a fellowship, in which they were caught up into the life of their risen and exalted Lord.

Accordingly, in the Acts of the Apostles (often named 'the gospel of the Holy Spirit') and in the letters which the apostles wrote to the young churches they had founded, the Holy Spirit appears as the Enabler of Christians in their new life, their Enlightener in the truth of the gospel. But among the apostles *the* theologian of the Spirit was unquestionably St Paul. (See, for example, Gal. 5, I Cor. 12-14, Rom. 8.)

How various are the roles assigned to the Spirit in his letters! Illuminator, Bestower, Uniter, Assurer – he is all these in one. The Spirit bestows all spiritual gifts, of which the greatest is Christian love. He binds men together in Christian fellowship, aids them in their prayers, enables them to cry 'Abba, Father'. Apostles he empowers to know the 'mind' (i.e. the intention) of Christ. 'Love, joy, peace' and 'every virtue we possess' (as the hymn has it) are the Spirit's gracious fruits in Christian living. And, as it was the Spirit of God which took his Son out of the grave, so that same

43

Spirit, indwelling us, is the 'earnest' – the pledge and first instalment – of the heavenly glory God has in store for his redeemed children.

II

Such was the Holy Spirit in those far-off days when in Carlyle's phrase, 'the hallowed fire flew from soul to soul', and one loving heart set another aflame.

Now come down the centuries and survey the Christian scene today. No honest observer can deny that much of the 'geist' (which is German for 'spirit') has gone out of our Christianity, and that for lack of it we are in peril of becoming 'God's frozen people'.

In face of this religious decline our church leaders now bravely address themselves to the task of re-shaping the church's structure, devising new ministries, and redeploying her shrinking resources and man-power. All honour to them for their courageous planning! But is it enough? What will it profit us if, with all our reorganizing, we have lost the Spirit which once drove the young church into a 'hard, pagan world', conquering and to conquer?

Happily signs are not lacking that some Christians are beginning to recognize their true need.

Thus, the Holy Spirit, so long 'the theologians' step-child' (Brunner) begins again to engage their interest and concern, as witness Charles Raven's *The Creator Spirit* and John V. Taylor's *The Go-between God*.[2] The first reminds us that our God is the God of nature as well as of grace, and that God's Spirit is to be seen at work not only in the story of our redemption but also in the long travail of evolution (Rom. 8.8-15 was his favourite passage in Paul). Taylor, starting from what may be called 'a natural theology' of the Spirit, writes refreshingly of the Holy Spirit as 'the anonymous Third Party', or Medium in our midst, who unseals our eyes not only to God's glory in his world but to his great grace in Christ.

Yet more significant, in our view, has been the spread over the world in our generation of the Pentecostals who in their own – often uncouth – way have recovered the lost power of the Spirit. Criticize them as we may – and many deprecate their obsession with 'speaking in tongues' and are uneasy about their doctrine of 'second baptism' in the Spirit – none may deny that the Pentecostal movement registers a salutary protest against an overly 'cerebral' Christianity, that it has revitalized many moribund churches, and that it has promoted warmer Christian fellowship.

Here is a point well worth our consideration. Nowadays the church's many critics never connect its worship with the note of joy.

Yet 'joy' in Paul's view comes second only to 'love' as a fruit of the Spirit, as joyfulness, born of the Holy Spirit, characterized Christianity in its early springtime. No less today is such joy in the Spirit the mark of the Pentecostals who, as statistics show, are now 'the fastest growing church in Christendom'. Is this merely fortuitous? Does it not rather spotlight one chief cause for 'the lost radiance' of contemporary Christianity? (We err if we think of the Spirit as the peculiar possession of our charismatic brethren. According to the New Testament, it belongs to all who can say, 'Jesus Christ is Lord – my Lord'.) Can we not here learn from the Pentecostals?

Once, long ago, there came by night to Jesus in Jerusalem a teacher in Israel named Nicodemus, curious to know more about the religious revival then sweeping the land. 'What you need', Jesus told him, 'is such a re-orientation of your whole life as can only be compared to new birth.' 'Impossible!' replied the literal-minded Nicodemus. Then, as they walked, the night wind rustled about their place of meeting. 'Listen to the wind, Nicodemus!' said Jesus. 'Whence it comes and whither it goes is a mystery. Yet how real a power it is! So is God's Wind, the Spirit. Here is what you need.'

Are we not today, many of us, Nicodemuses? Is there not in Christ's little parable about the night wind a word of God for us today? For too long our churches in the West, in tune with the humanistic thinking of the day, have been drifting into a 'flat-tyre' Christianity, devoid of all spiritual dynamic. In its beginnings, the faith was not a humanistic, natural religion, and the time has now come to hark back to the ancient springs of power, to reopen the whole life and work of our churches to the supernatural impact of God's Spirit. Like the campaign for 'Morals without religion', our experiment in humanistic Christianity has failed.

Doubtless our traditional forms of worship are too stiff and starchy and need changing. But the prime desideratum is for a change in the hearts of worshippers which only the Holy Spirit can produce. If we will but expose ourselves anew to 'the Lord, the Life-giver', put ourselves afresh, so to speak, under his management, who knows what miracles of refreshment and renewal may yet be in store for the church of Christ?

Notes

1. David S. Cairns, *An Autobiography*, SCM Press 1950, p. 200.
2. C. E. Raven, *The Creator Spirit*, Hopkinson and Harvard University Press 1927; J. V. Taylor, *The Go-between God*, SCM Press and Fortress Press 1972.

10

The Church

What is the church? How prone many of us are to identify it with a building – our wonted place of worship; or a denomination – our own one; or a clerical class ('Here comes the church!' we say as the minister comes along). But the Christian church is something incomparably older and bigger. It has a lineage that goes back to God's ancient people Israel, with its patriarchs and prophets, and a mission which embraces all mankind. We may define it as *the new and true people of God called into existence by God's saving action in Christ, and now numbering in the earth some thousand millions*. The great company of Christian people dispersed throughout the world – a supranational divine society which includes folk of every race and colour – this, and nothing less, is the church, the church catholic, or universal.

Incidentally, why do we Protestants, dissenters from the Church of Rome, allow it to monopolize that noble word 'catholic'? Whatever our denomination, never in narrow loyalty to our own one, ought we to surrender our just claim to belong to 'the catholic church', the whole company of God's people that have been, are, or shall be, on earth and in heaven: one body, whose sole Head is Christ.

I

The Christian church began when Christ called, trained and sent out twelve men (the number, note, of the tribes in old Israel) to form the first fruits of the Israel-to-be, the new 'chosen people' living under God's fatherly rule, the coming of which was the burden of Christ's 'good news', and which he embodied in his own life and work.

As all began in Galilee, so all culminated in Jerusalem with a cross on a hill and an empty tomb. And when, at the Last Supper, with broken bread and outpoured wine, Christ gave his men a share in the blessings of God's 'new covenant' or dispensation (Jer. 31.31f.), the twelve sat round their Master as the nucleus of the new people of God which, seven weeks later, at Pentecost, was empowered for its great mission by Christ's promised gift of the Holy Spirit.

During his ministry Jesus had called it his Father's 'little flock' (Luke 12.32). After Pentecost, the young church soon acquired new titles for itself, each containing some facet of the truth: 'the household of God', 'the bride of Christ', 'the fellowship of the Spirit'. But the church's other and best-known name in the New Testament is 'the body of Christ.'

Why 'body'? A man's body is the instrument whereby he communicates with the external world. Now, as we have seen, the early Christians had a vivid sense of the living Christ present and working in their fellowship through the Holy Spirit. So Paul named the church 'the (working) body of Christ', i.e. a social organism composed of many members, or limbs, and carrying out Christ's purposes in the world as once his physical body had done in Galilee and Judaea. (If you wish to go into the theology of all this, study Paul's letter to the Ephesians with a good commentary, or read John Mackay's splendid book, *God's Order.*[1])

Most of us have met men who claimed that they could be perfectly good Christians without joining the church. (Question: what should we say of a man who told us he could be a perfectly good soldier without joining the army?) Not for one moment does the New Testament countenance this view. What the apostolic writers tell us is that to be a Christian is to be 'in Christ' (i.e. in faith-union with a living Lord) and that this means being a member of the society of which he is the risen reigning Head. As the notion of an unattached soldier is a nonsense, so is that of a 'maverick' Christian.

A man once said to the evangelist D. L. Moody, 'I don't see that I can't be as good a Christian outside the church as within it.' In answer, Moody stepped over to the fire, drew a burning coal from it with the tongs, and let it burn by itself. In silence the two men watched the coal smoulder and go out. 'I see', said the man, and the next Sunday went to church. All true Christian experience is experience gained, shared and matured in the fellowship of other Christians.

II

What is the church's *raison d'être*, the reason for its existence?

First, *to proclaim the good news of God in Christ and to offer up 'spiritual sacrifices' of prayers and praises*.

This we do at public worship when in hymns we acknowledge God's 'worth-ship' – declare his greatness and his grace – and pray to him in Christ's name, and as he taught us, and share in those sacred acts we call 'sacraments.'

The whole pattern of our worship should reflect the story of our redemption – whether (as in the Old Testament lesson) the preparation in old Israel for the gospel or (as in the New Testament lesson) its fulfilment in Christ and his church and the coming of the Spirit to 'guide us into all the truth'. And the sermon? If it is a true one – and not merely somebody making himself a public nuisance with his private opinions on some question of the day – it should concern itself with some aspects of God's unique self-disclosure, of which the Bible is the record, and its relevance for Christian belief and behaviour in the world of today. Finally, all our worship should end with the benedictory suggestion not just that we are being sent *away* but that we are being sent *out* to witness for the gospel in the world.

So to the church's second calling. We are saved into a society which has a mission to the whole human race. Therefore the church's role is to be *God's collective missionary to men*. This mission is not confined to the heathen overseas who still 'bow down to wood and stone'. It begins in the semi-pagan world around the church's doors, as it ought to be the urgent concern of all committed Christians. And here the witness of our own Christian lives in the community will bear more eloquent testimony to the gospel's truth than many sermons.

Third, the church has a duty to apply her holy faith to public conduct by providing *a moral guide to society*.

'You are the salt of the earth', Jesus told his disciples (Matt. 5.13): 'salt', to keep society wholesome and preserve it from moral decay. So it should be still for those who call Christ Lord. Most of the problems which vex mankind are, at bottom, moral. In the gospel we Christians have set before us standards for moral action far above those prevailing in 'the permissive society' around us. On us therefore is laid the obligation not only to defend Christian values whenever they are threatened but also to live lives worthy of our high calling.

III

All this presents a daunting challenge to Christians in a world where today society is very sick and the church's image badly tarnished. Matthew Arnold's saying[2] that 'men cannot do without Christianity, and yet they cannot do with it as it is', is still truer if for 'Christianity' we read 'the church'. Sadly we have to confess that the church is not what it ought to be. Its witness to the gospel is muted, its sense of mission feeble, its impact on our egoistic society minimal. Above all, the church is disunited. How all the schisms and sects

48

arose in Christendom is not for discussion here. What is clear is that there are deep wounds in what we have called Christ's working body, and that this state of affairs accords neither with our Lord's prayer that 'they all may be one' (John 17.21) nor with the apostle's doctrine ('There is one body and one Spirit', Eph. 4.4). More, our unhappy divisions stultify the church's mission at home and especially abroad. How, for example, do we answer converts from 'the Third World' who protest, 'Why force your divisions on us? Why can't we sit together with all our brother Christians at the Lord's table?'

Happily there has now begun to blow through most branches of the church a welcome 'wind of change'. Of this the Ecumenical Movement and the World Council of Churches are the encouraging first fruits. Christians, so long content to shelter behind their own denominational barriers, are beginning to realize that God is calling them today to recover their lost unity, and so present a common Christian front to the world.

Ticklish problems of church order (e.g. that of 'bishops in presbytery') still await settlement; but today our emphasis should be on the many things Christians hold in common rather than on the few things which keep them apart. Nor should thorny doctrinal questions be allowed to hold up the task of achieving *a working unity* in which all Christians, whatever their denominational labels, can co-operate to form a 'United States' of the Church.

Let us start at the grass roots, as there are signs some are now doing, with Roman Catholics and Protestants working together in a community for the common Christian good. Protestants will rightly continue to challenge Rome's claim to be the only true church of Christ. Yet they might well take their marching orders from the good Pope John. 'Whenever I see a wall between Christians', he said, 'I try to pull out a brick.'

Here is a 'Go and do thou likewise' for all who call themselves Christians.

Notes

1. J. A. Mackay, *God's Order; the Ephesian Letter and this Present Time*, Nisbet and Macmillan, New York, 1953.

2. Matthew Arnold, *God and the Bible*, Smith, Elder & Co. and Macmillan, New York, 1875, p. 372.

II

The Sacraments

What are sacraments? We may define them generally as social actions which, appealing to the soul through the senses (like great music, painting or sculpture) convey spiritual grace and truth. There is nothing older in the New Testament than the two sacraments of baptism and the Lord's Supper. One is the rite of initiation into the church of Christ, the other that of ongoing fellowship in it.

These sacraments are the acted word of God, the gospel made *visible*, as in true preaching it is made *audible*. They are God's message for the eye – indeed for the whole body – expressed in everyday acts – washing with water, eating bread and drinking wine – which all men can understand.

The sacraments symbolize God's mercy – not magic, as if they were spiritual prophylactics against all evil. (Paul drives this point home in I Cor. 10.1-5.) It is from Christ's atoning death for our sins that both derive their efficacy which, at the font or the holy table, is, by the Holy Spirit's working, delivered home (so to speak) to our address.

No bare signs, the sacraments are *energetic* symbols, symbols which convey to men of faith what they signify – the grace of God in his crucified and living Son.

I

It is an old delusion which dies hard that baptism is the rite in which 'the baby gets its name'. In fact, it is the parents who give the name sometimes after long domestic argument. We call a child's first name its Christian one because it is customary to utter it at its christening. But the sacrament would be just as valid if the name were never spoken.

Christian baptism, as we said, draws its virtue from what God did for men in Christ's cross, and means being brought into Christ's fellowship, which is the church.

According to the New Testament, all men have in principle received baptism long ago, namely on Golgotha, on Good Friday and at Easter. There the essential act of baptism was carried out, without our co-operation, and even without our faith.[1]

To understand this deep doctrine, let us recall that Christ himself had described his atoning death as his baptism (Luke 12.49; Mark 10.38f.). It was a baptism in blood for men's saving, appointed for him by his heavenly Father. (This doctrine of baptism is traceable through the whole New Testament.) When therefore we are baptized, we are made to share in that act by which God, in principle, redeemed our sinful race and which, through his Holy Spirit, he now makes available for all who will.

Here is the same point made in some anonymous words[2] which we cannot better:

The most dramatic moment at the beginning of the ministry of Jesus was when He stood in Jordan to be baptised along with a mixed crowd of sinful men. This baptism was for the remission of sins – but He had no sin. It was 'for repentance' – but He was repenting not for His own sins but for the sins of the whole world of men.

A most dramatic moment came towards the end of Jesus' ministry when He said, 'I have a baptism to be baptised with' – meaning His death on the Cross. This is why we are baptised – so that we may have 'the remission of sins', the forgiveness of God, which Christ accomplished for us on the Cross. Its purpose is that we may be 'in Christ', taken up into his repentance for us, and into all that he has won for us. We become part of him, and members of His Body, which is the Church. We are named as his.

If this 'theology of Christian baptism' should prove too 'deep' for some, then let us liken baptism to what in political terms is called 'naturalization'. Before a man becomes a naturalized citizen of a country, he may have lived in it for years, shared its life, absorbed its traditions. But 'naturalization' makes him a full citizen of that country with all its privileges, so that the nation's king becomes his king in a sense impossible before. Just so, in baptism, our parents take out for us 'letters of naturalization' in the divine commonwealth, the church, of which Christ is King and Head.

In this illustration we have had in mind infant baptism. But not a few good Christians known as 'Baptists' hold that the sacrament should only be administered to adults on conscious profession of their faith. (How, they ask, can babes in arms possibly understand what is happening to them at the baptismal font? Do not some of them in fact seem vocally to register their dissent?)

Christians who are not Baptists agree that the church must provide baptism for those who, unchristened as children, as adults profess their faith in Jesus Christ as Lord and Saviour. Yet they also hold that infant baptism has at its back good Christian warrant.

First, in New Testament times whole households were baptized, and these must have included children. Next, in infant baptism it is the *parents' faith* that matters; but, by the judgment of Christ himself (recall the story of the paralytic who was brought by his four friends to Jesus for healing (Mark 2.1-12), such *vicarious* faith can avail for others. And, third, baptism *unto* faith has as good right in the principle of the gospel where grace *precedes* faith as baptism *upon* faith.

'Suffer the little children to come unto me, and forbid them not', said our Lord to his disciples. It cannot then be unchristian to cast the mantle of God's grace over a child in his tender years, provided that we also insist that his Christian initiation will not be complete till, grown to years of discretion, he confirms for himself, by public profession, the vows which his parents once took on his behalf.

II

So to the sacrament of continuing fellowship in the church. All our celebrations of the Lord's Supper run back to the Last Supper (Mark 14.17-25; I Cor. 11.23-26), itself in origin a Passover meal. At the high point in that feast, when devout Jews ate the Passover lamb with unleavened bread and drank wine, recalling Israel's deliverance from Egyptian bondage, Jesus gave the bread and wine the *new* meaning which transformed it into the Christian Lord's Supper. Breaking the bread, he gave it to the disciples, saying, 'Take, this is (represents) my body (myself)'. Then, handing them the cup, full of red wine, he declared, 'This is my blood of the (new) covenant, which is poured out for many.'

By describing the broken bread and the outpoured wine as his 'body' and 'blood', Jesus was portraying, in vivid symbol, that sacrifice of his own sinless life soon to be completed on Calvary's hill. By inviting the twelve to partake of the bread and wine (so interpreted), he was giving them 'a share in the power of the broken Christ' – making over to them in advance that sacrifice of himself which he was making once for all to God.

So the Lord's Supper (or Eucharist) began, as down the centuries it has been a trysting-place for Christians with their Lord. What should it mean for us today? It would be hard to improve upon the answer given by Principal David Cairns: 'a retrospect, and a prophecy, with renewal of the covenant face to face.'

First, 'retrospect', looking back, remembering in obedience to Christ's command, 'This do in remembrance of me', that is, 'for my recalling.' Not therefore remembering in the sense in which, every 25th of January, Scotsmen keep 'the immortal memory' of Robert Burns. (How can we have such a 'memorial' of one who is still alive, still our life?) No, remembering in the Bible's *dynamic* sense of making the past live again in the present, as suggested in the negro spiritual's question, 'Were you there when they crucified my Lord?' If we remember aright, the cross steps out of its frame in past history. We are 'there' with the twelve in the upper room on 'the night in which he was betrayed'. We are 'there' with the women before the gaping tomb on the first Easter morning to hear again the tremendous tidings, 'He is risen!'

Next, the Lord's Supper has a forward look. 'You proclaim the Lord's death until he comes', says St Paul. The Supper 'speaks to us softly of a hope'. It lifts our thoughts to Christ's coming in glory at the end, when God the Father will wind up the scroll of history, vanquish all evil powers, and Christ's people will be for ever at home in his Father's house.

Looking back, looking forward, memory and hope – but there is a third element in that sacrament which binds memory and hope together, and which alone entitles us to call it as we do 'Communion'. It is the real presence, through the Spirit, of the living Christ who comes, unseen but not unknown, to bless his people. The broken bread and the outpoured wine are, in Forsyth's fine phrase, 'Christ's love-tokens to his body, the church': signs which really convey what they symbolize, because, as long experience has shown, they deepen and enrich the spiritual bond between the Redeemer and his redeemed. So today Christ renews the new covenant once sealed with his own blood upon the cross.

Yet the renewing of the covenant is not his only. As we are Christ's faithful followers we renew it also, engaging ourselves to be better and truer members of his body, the church, and promising to fight ever more bravely against the world, the flesh and the devil to our life's end.

Notes

1. O. Cullmann, *Baptism in the New Testament*, SCM Press and Allenson 1950, p. 23.

2. *Life and Work*, January 1964, p. 19.

12

The Christian Ethic

When the backwoods preacher reminded his hearers that the gospel had a 'behaving' as well as a 'believing' side to it, he was referring to what we call 'the Christian Ethic'.

Ethic (or ethics) is the science of morals; and, like other sciences, there is more than one variety of it. Thus, those who find no room in their thinking for the supernatural opt, naturally enough, for 'naturalistic ethics'. But for Christians who believe in a greater world, transcending this one yet interpenetrating it, the moral imperative comes from beyond, from the living God as revealed in Christ. Christian ethics have therefore been defined as 'the science of human conduct as determined by divine conduct'. Yet, since Christianity is a divine life rather than a divine science, Christian behaviour in the New Testament is basically our human response in living to the grace of God. 'In the New Testament', said Erskine of Linlathen, 'religion is grace and ethics is gratitude.'[1]

I

The Greek philosophers had of course given grave thought to the question of what 'the good life' is. The Christian ethic, however, derives not from Aristotle and the Greeks but from Christ and his apostles. Moreover, though it presupposes and includes the Ten Commandments, it goes beyond them (see Matt. 5.21-48). For, as 'Christ brought all newness in bringing himself' (Irenaeus), so the way of life prescribed for his followers is new in various ways.

First, with Christ – and after him, his apostles – *it makes love the master-key to the problems of social relations.* (Most of Christ's commands in the gospels, e.g. 'give to him who asks', are but applications of the law of love to specific situations in daily life.) Unlike our word 'love' today (which can mean almost everything from Hollywood to heaven), *agapé*, the New Testament Greek word for it, is neither erotic nor sentimental. Study Christ's teaching in the Sermon on the

Mount (Matt. 5–7) or in his parables, and note how practically, unsentimentally, and all-embracingly he construes the verb to love. By 'loving' he means 'caring', caring actively and selflessly not only for the decent and the deserving but for all who need our help, even enemies. 'How can I love my neighbour when I don't know who he is?' asked the quibbling 'lawyer' in Christ's famous story (Luke 10.25–37). 'Real love', Christ answered him in effect, 'never asks questions like this. All it asks for is opportunities of going into action.'

Yet this is but half of 'love's story' in the gospels. If in his life Christ called for such selfless caring, by his death he gave the word 'love' a still richer meaning. There, at Calvary, the supreme act of *agapé* had been performed in history, so that henceforth his followers began interpreting it in terms of the Cross. 'Herein is love', wrote St John, 'not that we loved God but that he loved us, and sent his Son to be the expiation for our sins' (I John 4.10).

Accordingly, as A. C. Craig[2] has memorably said,

> The word love always needs a dictionary; and for us Christians the dictionary is Jesus Christ. He took this chameleon of a word and gave it a fast colour, so that ever since it is lustred by His teaching and life, and dyed in the crimson of Calvary, and shot through with the sunlight of Easter morning.

Here it is worth pausing to make a needed point about Christian love. When St John tells us, twice over, that 'God is love' (I John 4.8, 16), he does not mean that loving is only one of God's many activities. He means that *all* God's activity is loving activity. If he creates, he creates in love; if he rules, he rules in love; if he judges, he judges in love. In short, all God does is the expression of his nature which is – to love.

Now our Christian love is really God's love to us in Christ reflected and responded to. ('We love, because he first loved us.') It follows therefore that St Augustine's summary of the Christian love-ethic, 'Love, and what you will, do' means: 'If you hold your peace, through love hold your peace; if you cry out, through love cry out; if you correct, through love correct; if you spare, through love spare.' All our Christian activity, whether protesting, rebuking, sparing, or, on occasion, even just keeping our mouths shut – is, or ought to be, loving activity.

Still today in a world so very different from that of Christ and his apostles, such love ought to be the law of the Christian's living. Hard it will often be to apply in our complex society; but, as we seek to practise it, we shall find that it has a capacity to sweeten human relations and to make life's rough places plain which nothing else has.

In the second place, *the Christian ethic combines gladness in hardship with the promise of heavenly reward.*

You will hear this note sounding all through the New Testament, but its true source is our Lord's beatitudes (Matt. 5.3-12) where he pronounces 'divinely happy' all those whom the world pities, despises, and persecutes. This is a quite *new* note (as the Jew Claude Montefiore honestly acknowledged), and one that has characterized ever since Christianity's saints and martyrs, besides enabling countless sufferers to rise superior to their adversities. 'Radiance amid the strain and stress of life', as Baron von Hügel told the Quaker Rufus Jones, has ever been the absolutely essential mark of a true 'saint'; and perhaps there is no better example of it in the New Testament than Paul's prison letter to the Philippians with its 'Rejoice in the Lord always; again I will say, Rejoice' (Phil. 4.4).

Nor let any carping moralist tell us, *à propos* of the beatitudes, that 'virtue should be its own reward.' For Jesus promises reward to those who are obedient without thought of reward (Bultmann). 'Do good', he bids his followers, 'expecting nothing in return' (Luke 6.35) – a point unforgettably driven home in his parable of the Last Judgment (Matt. 25.31-46).

The third distinctive feature of the Christian ethic is that, *for its practice, it presupposes a fresh gift of divine power.* In the New Testament this gift is sometimes the Holy Spirit, and sometimes it is the living Christ. It is a distinction without a real difference, for the presence of the Spirit is really Christ himself present in spirit, the Christ of whom Paul wrote, 'I can do all things in (union with) him who strengthens me' (Phil. 4.13).

For Christians, then, Christ is 'the Lord of all good life', yet not simply as the past embodiment in a human life of perfect goodness. Ours is a living and ubiquitous Lord, 'the same yesterday, today and for ever'. He it is who leads us on our pilgrim way, as in him resides the strength needed for our journey. 'The living Christ', wrote T. W. Manson in his *Ethics and the Gospel*,' still has two hands, one to point the way, and the other held out to help us along';[3] and as we set out on our pilgrimage we are assured that he is with us 'to the end of time' (Matt. 28.20).

II

Such are the distinctive features of New Testament ethics. Space will not permit us to dwell here on the *inwardness* of Christ's moral teaching ('from within, out of the heart', Mark 7.21), or to show how he gave a new glory to the idea of humble service (John 13.1-17) or, by his word and example, exalted forgiveness and 'magnanimity' (*epieikeia*, John 8.1-11) in a way that none before him had ever quite done.

Today our problem is how to apply these gospel ethics to situations and circumstances which never came within the purview of Christ and his apostles. Thus, if the New Testament does supply guidance on what should be the *normal* attitude of the Christian to the civil power (Mark 12.13-17; Rom. 13.1-7; I Peter 2.13-17), it has little or nothing to say, as the continuing controversy between Pacifists and non-Pacifists shows, on the Christian attitude to war (Christ's saying, 'Love your enemies', refers to personal enmity).

Our task therefore becomes one of seeking, with the guiding principles of the gospel before us, and with the help of the Holy Spirit, to work out Christian answers to the many moral questions which now vex us. For the church has not only a duty to translate her holy faith into ethics relevant to the world we live in, but also the right to protest fearlessly against the evils which disfigure our society today.

Yet protests, by themselves, are not enough. What is required is some positive form of Christian action. What then should be the church's strategy in this holy war?

Some say that what we need is a Christian political party. (This is the Catholic principle, as witness the political parties on the Continent calling themselves 'Christian Democrats'.) Its proponents argue that the Bible, with its project in the Old Testament of a new national structure, and in the New of a new world order, viz., the kingdom of God, is in fact a political manifesto and a plan for such Christian moral action.

If some of us demur to this view, it is because we believe that no political 'set-up' is to be equated with the kingdom of God, and because no mere piety or personal holiness is a guarantee of political acumen or public sagacity.

There is another and, as we think, a better way. The church's duty, we hold, is not to solve 'social problems'. Her proper calling is to provide the men, the principles and the public which can. Accordingly, her aim should be to produce men and women who, adding Christian conviction and principle to their own professional expertise in business, industry and politics, will carry Christian cleanness of hand and purpose into the places where today the real power lies and the big decisions are taken. So best will the church fulfil her task of

57

bringing the gospel ethic into the world around her doors and prove herself the moral guide to society which she ought to be.

Notes

1. Quoted by R. N. Flew, *Jesus and his Way*, Epworth Press 1963, p. 13.
2. A. C. Craig, 'Rooted and Grounded in Love' in *The Sacramental Table*, ed. G. J. Jeffrey, James Clarke 1954, Harper Bros. 1955, p. 50.
3. T. W. Manson, *Ethics and the Gospel*, SCM Press 1960, p. 68.

13

This Life and the Next

'If a man die, shall he live again?' – thus Job posed the perennial question. The Christian answer is: 'I believe in the resurrection of the dead and the life everlasting.'

Christians of course are not the first or only people who have believed that 'the grave is not the goal'. No nation or tribe known to anthropologists but has believed in an after-life of one kind or another. And we may well ask, if, as many believe, death is the Everlasting No, striking man down finally to the dust, how it comes that there is this Everlasting Yea implanted in the human heart.

Moreover, down the centuries, philosophers have piled argument upon high argument to show that death does not write *finis* to man's story. From the incompleteness of human life (and especially all young lives tragically cut short), from the crying injustices of this world (and especially the sufferings of innocent people), from the greatness as well as the misery of man, they have concluded, 'There must be another existence where all lives will come to fruition, all wrongs be redressed, all mysteries be made plain.'

Thus, with no mention of Christ and the gospel, men have argued that somehow, somewhere, beyond the great divide of death there must be fuller and richer life. But Christianity has other and better arguments than these, and they are all bound up with Christ.

I

Christian belief in the life everlasting rests on two strong pillars.

The first is *the character of God as he has revealed himself to us in Christ*. We believe in a God whose nature is almighty love, a love that will not let us go, even in the dark valley of death.

Such, in substance, was Christ's reply to the Sadducees, the 'materialists' of his day, who held that 'dead men rise up never'. Once they put a question to him, hoping to catch him out (Mark 12.18-27). Though they themselves did not believe in an after-life, they knew that Christ did. The 'poser' they put was about a woman who had seven brothers in succession as her husbands. 'Now, suppose for argument's sake', they said, 'that there is an after-life, whose wife will she be in heaven?'

Jesus replied: 'You Sadducees know neither your own scriptures nor the power of God. Why, those very books of the Bible you accept as inspired scripture *imply* a future life. Moreover, in the resurrection-life men and women do not marry; their life is like that of the angels – one of perfect communion with God.' Then, quoting back at his critics their own scriptures, he said: 'Have you never read in the book of Moses, how God said to him, "I am the God of Abraham, the God of Isaac and the God of Jacob"? God is not God of the dead but of the living. You are quite mistaken.'

'Never', says our Lord in effect, 'never think of the living God as the mourner of his dead friends. A poor, impotent God he would be if he could not save his friends from death! And if God is the God of Abraham, of Isaac and of Jacob – if they are his men and he their God – they cannot be dead and done with. The Lord has need of them. Therefore they are alive now and in his almighty keeping.'

It is upon *the faithful love of God* that Christ rests everything. God called these men his friends, and God does not leave his friends in the dust. When God loves once, he loves for ever – loves in life, loves in death, loves beyond death. It is the same great argument with which St Paul crowns his supreme chapter, the eighth of his letter to the Romans: 'I am persuaded that neither death nor life . . . shall be able to separate us from the love of God which is in Christ Jesus our Lord.' Long ago St Augustine summed it up in a Latin epigram: *Quod Deo non perit, sibi non perit*, which may be roughly paraphrased, 'The friends of God do not perish.'

II

The second strong pillar is *the resurrection of Christ himself*.

When, on that first Good Friday, their Master hung lifeless on his cross, it must have seemed to his disciples that the finest life they had ever known had gone out in utter darkness. But, wonder of wonders, on the first Easter Day he had come back to them in glory. Somehow, by God's mighty act, Christ had left one gaping tomb in the wide graveyard of the world. And, as death had been for their Lord the gateway to new and more glorious life, so it would be for all who were his, for all who were 'in Christ.' With that hope the whole New Testament is radiant, as it throbs vibrantly through the modern ballad 'The Lord of the Dance':

They buried my body,
And they thought I'd gone,
But I am the Dance,
And I still go on.

They cut me down;
And I leapt up high;
I am the life
That'll never, never die,
I'll live in you,
If you'll live in me –
I am the Lord
Of the Dance, said he.[1]

III

We believe then that, in union with the living Christ (Rom. 8.17), we are heirs of everlasting life. But this is not all. With the men of the New Testament, we believe that God will one day consummate his kingdom, or saving rule, inaugurated in Christ, and judge and reward men according to the good or evil they have done in this life. To be in heaven will mean life in God's presence for ever; to be in hell will mean exclusion from that blessed life. (This is the one decisive feature, or factor, in the idea of hell – exclusion from the God who has made us for himself. 'The appropriate punishment for evil,' wrote Dean Inge, 'is not to be cooked in an oven, but to become incapable of seeing God, here or hereafter.'[2])

Who goes where? That there is such a thing as final exclusion from God's presence is the teaching of Christ and his apostles. But it is not for us to say upon whom this dread sentence may fall. (When Christ himself was asked, 'Are only a few to be saved?' he turned the question of theological curiosity into one of existential challenge: 'Few enough to make you afraid you may not be there,' he said in effect, 'See to your entry!' See Luke 13.23f.) What we may believe is that the Father of Christ will not suffer the sentence to fall on any who do not wilfully pronounce it upon themselves. The whole long debate about election and predestination has been admirably summed up by P. T. Forsyth: 'We are all', he said, 'predestined in love, to life, sooner or later – *if we will*.'

It is no part of Christian wisdom to presume detailed knowledge of either the furniture of heaven or the temperature of hell. Yet three things about the after-life the New Testament entitles us to affirm.

First, *the other life then is the other life now*. Eternity does not lie merely at the end of time; it pervades it now – 'beats at our own clay-shuttered doors'. Accordingly, every genuine Christian experience in this life is a sample in advance of the heavenly life:

> The men of grace have found
> Glory begun below.

This is what St John means by eternal life as a *present* experience, and St Paul when he calls the gift of the Holy Spirit an 'earnest' – a first instalment, or down payment, of our heavenly inheritance.

Second: when we die in union with Christ, *we pass into no lone immortality*. Life hereafter is a family life, a society of redeemed persons living for ever in the presence of God, his Christ and all the saints. The point is well made in that glorious hymn about the church triumphant, 'Jerusalem the golden', though its author, Bernard of Cluny, confessed, as we all must:

> I know not, O I know not
> What *social joys* are there,
> What radiancy of glory,
> What light beyond compare.

Third: *the nature of our resurrection life is given us in Christ's own*. Our hope is set not on 'a resurrection of relics' (as Paul makes clear in I Cor. 15.50) but upon a God-given 'spiritual body' – that is, an organism in which the fulness of personality will be preserved. What does this mean? It means that 'if I am a somebody now, an individual with a name, then, by God's goodness, I shall be the *same body* then.'[3]

When we talk about heaven, we must ever use the language of symbol. 'Paradise', or the garden of God, and 'Jerusalem the golden' are two such symbols used in the New Testament. But the best is that which our Lord used in the upper room: 'a Father's house with many rooms' (John 14.2 RSV). All three suggest a blessedness beyond all human telling.

In what Conan Doyle might have called 'the Case of the Doctor's Dog', it is told of a dying man that he asked his godly doctor to tell him something of the place to which he was going. As the doctor fumbled for his reply, there came a scratching at the room's door, and his answer was given him. 'Do you hear that scratching?' he asked his patient. 'It's my dog. I left him downstairs, but he has grown impatient and, hearing my voice, has come upstairs. He has no notion of what lies inside this door, but he knows that I am here. Isn't it the same with you? You do not know what lies beyond the door, but you know that your Master is there.'

Heaven, we believe, is the place where our Master now is, and, as we also believe, all those good and true souls whom we 'have loved long since and lost awhile'.

If all this is true, how much depends on our being united with Christ, here and now! Outwardly, men and women may all seem to be living the same kind of life; but inwardly and really, it is not so. Some are living only for the passing day and for its trumpery and transient pleasures. Others are living for eternity, because their lives are founded on faith in God through the living Christ. The question which the gospel puts to each one of us is this: 'What kind of life are you living? Are you a friend of God and a follower of his Son?'

Notes

1. The last lines of 'I danced in the morning' by Sydney Carter, quoted from *Songs of the Seventies*, Galliard Ltd and St Andrew Press 1972, no. 13; used by permission of Stainer and Bell Ltd.

2. W. R. Inge, *Christian Ethics and Modern Problems*, Putnam 1930, p. 75.

3. C. F. D. Moule, *Christianity Revalued*, Mowbray 1974, p. 69.

PART THREE

CHRISTIAN COROLLARIES

14

The First Thing in Knowledge

In the granite city of Aberdeen the motto of its university reads: *Timor Domini Initium Sapientiae*: 'The fear of the Lord is the beginning of wisdom'. So AV, RSV and NEB render the original Hebrew of Psalm 111.10 and Proverbs 1.7. But, for most of us, Dr Moffatt's translation puts the matter more tellingly: 'The first thing in knowledge is reverence for the Eternal.'

What the motto affirms is that only on the granite of true religion can we build aright the house of learning. It is a proposition which, though unacceptable to humanists (who want 'morals without religion') and Communists (who, with Marx, dismiss religion as 'the opium of the people'), long commended itself to our fathers and forefathers. Were they so sadly in error? It was no cleric speaking to his brief but that blunt, rough soldier the Duke of Wellington who declared, 'Educate men without religion, and you do but turn out clever devils.' Is there not abundant evidence in the present state of the world to corroborate the Duke's dictum?

I

But let us begin at the beginning.

Today in educational circles there is lively discussion about teaching methods, old and new, and we hear much about 'comprehensive education'. But the word 'comprehensive' has more than one sense, and how many are to be found today asking the question, What really deserves the name of 'comprehensive education' in that other sense? Let us put it this way. Should the teacher's aim be simply, by grounding his pupils in what are traditionally known as 'the three R's', to enable them, when they grow up, to *earn a living*? Or should

64

it be no less a part of his business to teach them *how to live*? In short, are we sure that in much that passes for education today there is a clearly-conceived sense of direction?

Let us begin with the centres of higher education, the universities. Years ago, Sir Walter Moberly, then chairman of the University Grants Committee, wrote a book with the title *The Crisis in the University*.[1] He was convinced that there was something radically wrong in our universities. This something sprang from the very nature of modern knowledge. As the cynic said, the trouble with modern knowledge is that it is like a certain lady's past – there is so much of it. And the result? Well, you can dress it up in all sorts of high falutin phrases like 'the fragmentation of studies'; but what it boils down to is just this – the tragic lack of any common philosophy of life to bind together our disparate scraps of knowledge and help the student to see life steadily and see it whole.

Of course this crisis in the university is only part of a much bigger crisis in the wider world beyond the campus where so many people have no clue to the meaning of life, no sense of what is for, or where it is going. Cleverness we have in plenty – the devil's plenty of it. But there is also a deep hunger for *meaning* in life – a hunger which, because it is being starved, is seeking *ersatz* substitutes for it in football, racing, bingo, alcohol and drugs.

Come back again to colleges and universities. One root of the trouble is that 'specialization' has gone to our heads. A specialist has been defined as 'one who knows more and more about less and less, and ends up by knowing everything about nothing'. And the spectacle confronting us in many a college is that of scores and scores of able men and women, each sedulously cultivating his (or her) own little tree of knowledge, but with precious little idea of what the wood as a whole looks like. The result is that year by year we are sending out thousands of young people expert in the language of their own specializations, but often ill equipped to be the leaders of their generation that they ought to be.

Can we really dignify this with the name of higher education? Is the sole function of a college or university to turn out competent technicians in the welfare state? What will it profit our young men and maidens if, at the end of their courses, they are still mentally 'displaced persons' with no clear faith or philosophy of life to light them through a dark world?

II

Such is the situation today. How shall we remedy it? Where shall we find a worthy view of life for lack of which much modern education is a Joseph's coat of many colours with no dominant pattern running through it?

Should we, as some would persuade us, look hopefully to Communism? Is Marxism 'in widest commonalty spread' the answer? Do we seriously suppose that the religion of economic determinism with its concept of history as the unending anger of class against class, its ruthless disregard of the rights of the individual, its stifling of freedom and its psychiatric prisons for all thinkers who diverge from 'the party line' – that such a system will ever meet our need? If you want an answer, ask Solzhenitsyn.

Well, if not Communism, what about humanism with its specious offer of 'morals without religion'? Will humanism, with its doctrine of man 'the thinking reed' rooted in an unthinking universe, put meaning into meaningless lives and inspire to nobler living? Nay, has not history shown that in the great scale of things religion and morals hang together, and that, if you let the one go, the other will quickly follow it? Is not this what is happening today? How long, do you think, we can live on a creed which proclaims, 'Be good – although there is no Soul of Goodness at the heart of things'?

Communism, humanism – do these exhaust our choices? Is there not another and older and better alternative – the creed, the way of life, which we call Christian?

III

You cannot prove Christianity true as you would prove a proposition in Euclid. There is such a thing as 'Christian certainty', but it is of another kind. But what the great Christians from St Paul and St John onwards promise is that, if we make the venture of Christian faith, the mysteries of this world will become mysteries not of darkness but of *light*.

But suppose Christianity true. Suppose the last reality in the universe is not man but the living, loving God of the New Testament who has revealed his grace and truth in Jesus Christ to men. Suppose it true that all our ideals come from this God, from his will prompting and claiming us. Suppose that behind the hurly-burly of history there is an unseen and eternal kingdom of God which, in spite of man's sinning, he, the Lord of history, is carrying forward to a blessed conclusion. Suppose too that when you have messed up your life and betrayed your ideals, this God does not give you up but is ready to offer you another chance – forgive you, accept you, and even use you in his purpose for the world. And suppose, finally, that this purpose of God's does not end with death but runs out, beyond this earthly scene, into a better world than this.

All these 'supposings' add up to what Christians believe. If, to use the old phrase, you 'decide for Christ', you are not promised answers to all the questions which have vexed thinking men down the centuries. There is plenty of room in Christianity for a healthy agnosticism. St Paul, who knew more about God and his Christ than any of us, could write, 'Our knowledge is imperfect ... Now I know only in part' (I Cor. 13.9-12). But he could also write, 'I know whom I have believed' (II Tim. 1.12), and 'I am persuaded that neither death nor life, nor angels nor principalities nor powers, nor things present nor things to come, nor height nor depth, nor anything else in all creation, shall be able to separate us from the love of God which is in Christ Jesus our Lord' (Rom. 8.38f.).

Here then is a creed centred in a Person, the unchanging Christ (Heb. 13.8), which makes sense of the world's riddle, which sees our human life as a kind of education which God our Father puts us through that we may be fit persons to enjoy all those blessed things he has in store for us, which regards men and women not just as cattle of a superior breed but as sons and daughters of the All Highest, and which finds the essence of the good life in the golden rule (Matt. 7.12) and the law of love and the summons to selfless service.

What real rival to this faith is there worth talking about? Why should we not insist on our children learning about it in the day school from Christians properly qualified to teach it in all its grace and grandeur? And, for a final consideration, do we really see this warring world of ours ever settling down on any other basis than the Christian doctrine of the fatherhood of God – that Father who still today is seeking in Christ his crucified and living Son to reconcile us to himself and out of the sinful and distracted children of men to create a single new humanity?

Note

1. Sir Walter Moberly, *The Crisis in the University*, SCM Press and Macmillan, New York, 1949.

15

Christian Discipleship

The only 'saints' the New Testament knows anything about are forgiven sinners. Begin with the first disciples. May we not all take comfort and hope when we remember that the twelve, whom Jesus called to be the first fruits of his church, were very frail and fallible folk, all too often motivated, as we are, by egoism or self-interest?

No clearer proof of this can be found than Mark's story about James and John, the sons of Zebedee, when the twelve were on their way up to Jerusalem, with Jesus a great lonely figure striding ahead of them, the physical gulf between them and him a fit symbol of the still greater spiritual gulf (Mark 10.32-45).

The story about 'the sons of thunder' (as Jesus nicknamed them – for the reason why, see Luke 9.51-56) is the story of a thoroughly selfish request by two of Christ's closest disciples. Once – we do not know precisely when – Jesus had promised the twelve a position of privilege in his heavenly kingdom (Matt. 19.28; Luke 22.30). Now, James and John, uncontented by this assurance, desire Jesus to promise them the two chief places in it. No wonder, as Mark tells us, these two place-seekers roused the indignation of the other ten!

'You don't know what you are asking', Jesus answered James and John, 'Can you drink of the cup that I am drinking and be baptized with the baptism I am baptized with?' He meant the cup of suffering his Father had ordained for him and the baptism of blood he must undergo if the holy fire of the gospel were to be kindled in the world (Luke 11.49).

Without a tremor of hesitation James and John answered: 'We can.' And, to our astonishment, Jesus took them at their word. 'You shall indeed drink my cup', he said; but he added that the gift of the chief places in 'glory' was in higher hands than his.

The sons of Zebedee had no idea what they were really asking. Why then did Jesus take them at their word? What thinking lay behind his acceptance of their bold 'We can'? Was it not this oft-forgotten truth that if a master is going to do anything at all with his disciples, he must, to begin with, accept them as they are? If they pledge themselves in their own terms, provided they are sincere, this is enough – enough at any rate for a start.

Let us consider this truth, first from the angle of the master and then from the angle of the disciple.

I

In human affairs there must ever be an element of tension and cross purposes between a master and his followers. This it is which makes leadership – say, in politics or in war – so often a lonely and heart-breaking business. To be a true leader, you must be ahead of your followers, yet not too far ahead. Somehow you must contrive to live in your own world, and yet at the same time in theirs. You must be ready for loneliness, and yet retain liaison with your followers.

Judge, then, how formidable was our Lord's task with his twelve chosen men. One thinks, for instance, of Caesarea Philippi and the man on whom Jesus said he would build his church (Matt. 16.18). 'You are the Messiah', said Peter to Jesus speaking for the others. But when Jesus went on to tell them that messiahship for him meant a cross, 'Never!' responded Peter and began to rebuke his Master. 'Out of my sight, you Satan!' replied Jesus, 'You think as men think, not as God thinks' (Mark 8.33).

Even at last in the garden of Gethsemane (Luke 22.35-38) the irony of Christ's saying about 'buying a sword' was quite lost on Peter and the rest, who at once whipped out two swords, so that Jesus said sadly, 'Enough, enough.'

But if Christ's task with his disciples sometimes almost moved him to despair, consider also how great was his achievement in succeeding in it – succeeding in carrying his disciples over from their own little world in which ambition was a ruling motive, into his own great world in which ambition did not count and 'whoever would be first among you must become the servant of all' (Mark 10.44), succeeding in turning that handful of frail and sinful men into what the *Te Deum* calls 'the glorious company of the apostles'. And the secret of his success? Was it not because, initially, he took them as they were?

Here is food for thought for those called to be Christian leaders today. The Christian church, interpreting the world's riddle in the light of Christ, and finding in him its supreme exemplar, cherishes values and professes standards far ahead of and above the world's. Those therefore who hold office in it must beware of making the error of so many high-minded idealists in their efforts to improve and uplift humanity. It is the mistake of 'going all moral and spiritual high-brow' – of wanting to carry people off into a rarified spiritual atmosphere to which they are quite unaccustomed, of leaving them with no option except to be very bad or very good.

For an instance, a man may express a desire to join the church. Some well-meaning Christian may then tell him that, if he does, he must subscribe to (say) the Apostles' Creed, go to church every Sunday, read his Bible regularly, and so on. He refuses to join – he says it is too much. Would it not be wiser to ask him if he could accept some short and simple formula of Christian belief (like James Denney's 'I believe in God through Jesus Christ, His only Son, our Lord and Saviour'[1]) and whether he was honestly resolved to try to lead a Christian life?

This way you may win him; the other way you may not. And if any reader should protest that this is a very small Christian beginning, we may remind him of Christ's parable of the tiny mustard seed which grows taller than any other plant, so that the wild birds can nest in its shade (Mark 4.30-32; Luke 13.18), that is, we have dominical warrant for believing that 'small beginnings may have great endings'.

II

Now consider the issue from the disciples' angle. When James and John answered Christ's question with their bold 'We can', there were two elements in their promise which need examining: (*a*) an element of ignorance – they did not know what they were asking; and (*b*) an element of wrong motive – each had his weather eye open on the best place in Christ's coming 'glory'. Yet Christ took them at their word, took them as they were, because in their ignorant and wrongly motivated promise he discerned the hope, the potential, of nobler things; and, as history was to show, his trust in them was not misplaced.

(*a*) Dwell, first, on the element of ignorance, for it concerns us still today.

Many people today refuse the yoke of Christian discipleship (the metaphor is Christ's, see Matt. 11.29) because they fear that, if they assume it, they will not be able to keep their promise fully. 'When I make a promise', they will explain, 'I like to keep it; and, rather than not keep it, I won't promise.'

Honesty? Yes, but honesty of a very myopic sort. Better far to say, 'I can – I will – follow Christ' and then go on to learn, perhaps through much struggle and travail, a deeper knowledge of self and of Christ's power as Saviour.

All Christian discipleship starts in ignorance. Yet, unless in our ignorance, we are ready to make the venture of faith, we shall never find the riches – 'the unsearchable riches', Paul calls them (Eph. 3.8) – which all the saints have found in Christ. Here, as elsewhere, it is a case of 'Nothing venture, nothing win', and only as we make the venture, will the living Christ reveal himself to us so that we learn in fellowship with him who and what he is. Sydney Lysaght has said it all in his poem:

> If Love should count you worthy, and should deign
> One day to seek your door and be your guest,
> Pause ere you draw the bolt and bid him rest,
> If in your old content you would remain . . .
> He wakes desires you never may forget,
> He shows you stars you never saw before,
> He makes you share with him, for evermore,
> The burden of the world's divine regret.
> How wise you were to open not! And yet
> How poor if you should turn him from the door![2]

(b) Now take the element of wrong motive.

Some Oxford dons once fell to discussing the question, 'What is it that takes a man into the Christian ministry?' Manifestly it was not love of money. Then someone suggested that it was 'the desire to find a platform on which to strut before the public'.

Sometimes it may be so, though one hopes not often. Yet it does not matter two straws whether one of the man's motives may have been a love of the limelight, provided also that he has a genuine conviction that Christ is the master-light of all his spiritual seeing, the one 'real and living way' to the Father (John 14.6, Moffatt). And that he is likely to have had some such conviction is shown by the fact that the man has chosen the ministry, and not (say) the stage or politics which nowadays promise a much surer public platform on which to 'strut'. A man may begin with motives which are far from pure, but perseverance in the Christian Way may be trusted to refine them.

So with us all. Let is wait until our motives are quite pure before becoming Christ's liegemen, and we may wait till doomsday. 'If God were a Kantian', says C. S. Lewis somewhere, 'who would not have us till we came from the purest motives, who could be saved?' But if, even with our mixed motives, we venture our allegiance and seek, in strong earnest, to be his true disciples, in the end we may hope in Christ for what all the saints have hoped –

But that toil shall make thee
Some day all Mine own, –
And the end of sorrow
Shall be near My throne.[3]

Let the last word belong to George Macdonald (whom C. S. Lewis
called master in things spiritual); 'Christ is easy to please, but hard
to satisfy.' As long ago he accepted the brash 'We can' of James and
John, so Christ today accepts our miserable best, but upon that he
insists on building his own.

Notes

1. James Denney, *Jesus and the Gospel*, Hodder & Stoughton and Doran
1908, p. 398.
2. Sydney Lysaght, 'The Penalty of Love', *Poems*, Macmillan 1928, p. 33.
As in George Herbert's poem, 'Love bade me welcome', 'Love' stands for
'Christ'.
3. From the hymn 'Christian, dost thou see them, . . .' by St Andrew of
Crete, translated by J. M. Neale.

16

Christian Certainty

You cannot read the New Testament intelligently without perceiving that the early Christians were sure about three things. They were sure that there was a God who cared about the world he had made. They were sure that in one Man, Jesus Christ, God had acted decisively for us men and for our salvation. They were sure that his Holy Spirit was now powerfully at work amongst them, helping them to lead new and better lives.

God the Father almighty, Christ the Saviour, the Holy Spirit the Helper – these are still central certainties for Christians today. But what kind of certainty is theirs?

I

In this science-dominated age this is a question to which thinking Christians ought to have an answer. So spectacular have been the achievements of modern physics, astronomy, biology and medicine that many people today apparently believe that nothing has a claim to truth which cannot be proved by scientific experiment – like that of the chemist in his 'lab'.

But then the question arises: Is such science the only road to truth and certainty? 'Science' is simply the 'Englished' form of the Latin word for 'knowledge' (*scientia*), and there is more than one form of knowledge by which what is knowable can be known. Certainties there are that natural science knows nothing of, as the great French scientist Blaise Pascal[1] testified. To him certainty came through a revelation not unlike that made to St Paul on the Damascus Road. Here is his own record of it:

> The year of grace 1654,
> Monday 23 November . . .
> From about half past ten in the evening until
> about half past twelve midnight.
> Fire.

'God of Abraham, God of Isaac, God of Jacob',
not of the philosophers and scholars.
Certitude, Certitude, emotion, joy, peace.
God of Jesus Christ[2].

Other kinds of certainty there are, then, which have a valid truth-claim. Here are four examples, each genuine in its own way but each different in kind from the others:

I am certain that two plus two make four.

I am certain that the Scots beat the English at Bannockburn in 1314, and lost to them at Flodden in 1513.

I am certain that William Shakespeare is a greater poet than William McGonagall.

I am certain of the love of my wife.

On these four matters I am tolerably certain, but in each case the reason for my certainty is different in kind. The historian cannot justify his certainty about an event like the battle of Bannockburn by mathematical proof. The literary critic cannot prove Shakespeare a greater poet than McGonagall by using a computer. And that husband would be a great ass who tried to demonstrate his love for his wife, or hers for him, by the rules of logic.

Does this mean that the lover is less justified in his certainty than the logician? Or that the historian or literary critic is less justified in his certainty than the mathematician? No, all it means is that, because they are dealing with different things, their methods must inevitably differ. Each man – mathematician, historian, logician, literary critic, lover – has his own kind of certainty.

II

Now take a further step. What is the supreme sort of certainty? The believer will answer: *religious* certainty; and if asked why, will reply, Because true religion embraces the whole of life, and not just a part of it. Accordingly, we should not be surprised if religious faith offers a different sort of certainty from that offered by, say, logic or mathematics.

What kinds of certainty is it? If you have ever experienced what it is to be loved by another human being, you have a valuable clue to its nature. Between the certainties of human love and the certainties of religious faith there is a real analogy or likeness. To be sure, our faith in God (or in Jesus Christ the God-man) is not the same as our faith in another human being. Yet the certainties of faith are more like those of human love than anything else in our experience.

What then is the important thing which the human lover and the lover of God have in common? What both alike are certain of is not a truth but a Person. Take St Paul. None knew the truths of the Christian religion better, as none could expound them more ably – witness his *magnum opus*, the epistle to the Romans – but what Paul was really sure of was not a truth but a Person, the risen Christ who, ever since he had appeared to him on the Damascus Road, had become the master-light of all his spiritual seeing and living:

> Yea, thro' life, death, thro' sorrow and thro' sinning,
> He shall suffice me, for He hath sufficed,
> Christ is the end, for Christ was the beginning,
> Christ the beginning, for the end is Christ.[3]

And therefore when Paul wrote to his young colleague Timothy he did not say, 'I am persuaded of the sovereign truths of our Christian religion.' What he wrote was: 'I know *whom* I have believed' (I Tim. 1.12).

So it has ever been down the Christian centuries. A modern instance is the great Scottish church leader, John White. In a broadcast recorded a day or two before he died, John White revealed how he had arrived at Christian certainty. It had not come to him, he explained, through abstract logical reasoning (e.g. by study of the classical proofs for God's existence) but by confrontation. 'I met a Man', he said. 'He revealed to me the grace and truth of God in a human life. And there is nothing so convincing as Truth and Love clothed in flesh and blood.'

St Paul and John White were essentially at one. Said Paul: 'The life I now live in the flesh I live by faith in the Son of God who loved me and gave himself for me' (Gal. 2.20). It was the same divine love confronting John White in the Man Jesus which made him the stalwart Christian that he was.

III

It is worthwhile dwelling a little longer on this analogy between human love and Christian faith in God.

Many things there are which a man may not know about his wife, yet he may be as sure of her as he is sure that the interior angles of a triangle are equal to two right angles. So there are many things which a Christian does not know about God, and yet, thanks to the fact of Christ, he may be sure about God and his grace. For what nature is to the scientist, that Christ is to the Christian believer. The New Testament Christ – the Christ who died for our sins and rose again, and now comes, unseen but not unknown, through the Holy Spirit – is the source of his certainty, and that certainty has a title to be called 'scientific' because it has been tested and found true in ongoing Christian experience.

Christian certainty like this is quite compatible with what has been called 'theological illiteracy'. Ask many a mature Christian if he is sure about his faith. He will assure you that he is. Proceed to 'quiz' him about his assurance. Ask him if he can shed light on the mystery of the incarnation, how God became man in Christ. Or invite him to explain the Christian doctrine of 'God in three Persons, Blessed Trinity'. He will be completely at a loss for answers. Yet, though weak on doctrine, he will stay unshakably sure about the Person – the living Christ who is at the centre of his Christian life.

Christians, then, have a real and justifiable certitude about their faith. Of course there are many things in the world (like cancers and earthquakes) which they cannot account for, as there are many things about God on which they are content to remain 'agnostic'. But for them, thanks to Christ's coming, the world's mysteries have become mysteries not of darkness but of *light*, and by that light they travel, asserting against all unbelievers, 'God cares for me, Christ died for me, the Holy Spirit helps me.' And what is this but the burden of all the great Christian creeds and confessions?

IV

Thus far we have established two things. First, there are other certainties besides those of science. Second, Christian faith, which for us is the supreme certainty, finds its best analogy in human love. For what both the human lover and the lover of God have in common, and are certain of, is not a truth but a person.

Yet there remains a something else which must be mentioned in any true account of Christian certainty. George Macdonald somewhere defines true religion as holding on to God with one hand while we stretch out the other one to help our brother. Vivid as this definition is, it says nothing about that 'something else' which comes first in all Christian certainty. Paul had it in mind when he wrote, 'God shows his love for us in that while we were yet sinners Christ died for us' (Rom. 5.8). So had Pascal in his paradox: 'You would not seek Me if you had not already found Me.'[4] It is the theme of Francis Thompson's tremendous poem, *The Hound of Heaven*. Our forefathers called it 'the prevenient grace of God'. In plain terms, we

76

can only hold on to God – be sure of him – because he himself has laid hold of us in Christ. ('Lay hold of', 'arrest' is the meaning of the Greek verb which Paul uses in Phil. 3.12)

Think of Christian faith in terms of what the Americans call a 'cinch'. Originally, a 'cinch' was a saddle-girth, the band which holds the horse's saddle in place. Our Christian faith is such a spiritual 'cinch', but only because, in Christ, God first made and fixed that securing band. The source of our certainty is not that we have found God but that God in his Son has found us and claimed us as his own.

Therefore

> Let me no more my comfort draw
> From my frail hold of Thee,
> In this alone rejoice with awe;
> Thy mighty grasp of me.[5]

Notes

1. Pascal invented the computer (*la machine arithmétique*) and the barometer, and solved the problem of the vacuum.

2. Pascal's *Pensées*, trans. M. Turnell, Harvill Press and Harper & Row 1962, no. 737 (the numbers follow the edition of L. Lafuma).

3. F. W. H. Myers, 'Saint Paul', *Collected Poems*, Macmillan 1921, p. 144.

4. Pascal, *Pensées*, no. 751 (in the Everyman edition, 1908, no. 554).

5. J. C. Shairp, *Glen Desseray and Other Poems*, Macmillan 1888, p. 265.

17

Christian Optimism

Mankind may be divided into two classes – the pessimists and the optimists. Like, for example, Thomas Carlyle and his American friend, R. W. Emerson. Unable to shake Emerson's incorrigible optimism, Carlyle took him the round of London's horrors, (ending up at the House of Commons!) and asked him, after each exhibition, 'Do you believe in the devil now?'

Neither the prophet of Ecclefechan nor the sage of Concord had realized that there was a third and better option open to them, a view of man and the world which does better justice to the patchwork of good and evil called history. We mean 'Christian optimism', with the stress upon the adjective. There is no spiritual commodity the world needs more today.

But first let us face the facts.

In the halcyon days of Queen Victoria it seemed to many that with the onward march of science man was advancing irresistibly to perfection. What was evil but a 'hang-over' from our animal ancestry, and sin but the stock-in-trade of an outmoded theology? The worst was over; at last man was out of the woods, and his future shone with unlimited promise.

Need it be said that to this bland optimism we have now said a long goodbye? By the two colossal disasters of the twentieth century and their awful aftermaths we have learned in blood and tears how dread a laboratory of good and evil is the heart of man. The grim logic of events has shattered the myth of man's natural goodness and shown (as the late Dick Crossman said) that there is a good deal more evidence in the world today for the Christian dogma of original sin than there is for the Marxist doctrine of the classless society.

So, over the globe, there hangs a deep spiritual depression; violence and vandalism, corruption and pornography, are on the increase; racial tensions and the fear of nuclear holocaust make the headlines of the news; and the best efforts of earnest men to set the world aright seem destined to go down before the resistless might of evil. Small wonder that many Christians who thought they had done with the devil have begun to take him seriously again.

Moreover, many are not only obsessed by the fears and perils of the day, but they almost think it is their Christian duty to be obsessed by them. Otherwise, people might take them for starry-eyed optimists who have lost touch with grim reality.

But let us ask: Is this a Christian frame of mind? Is it right that the professed followers of Christ should confront the world with heavy hearts and funereal faces?

It is recorded that Martin Luther once allowed himself to fall into a deep depression. For three days and nights he continued in the blues. On the fourth morning his wife appeared at the breakfast table dressed in deep mourning. Even the distracted Luther noted the change and asked her who had died. She replied, 'I thought from your behaviour for the last three days that the dear God himself had died.'

On this occasion the wife was a much better Christian than her redoubtable husband. For, while we Christians have no right to ignore the woes and heartaches of the world, equally we have no right to appear as Christ's lugubrious messengers to men. 'When you fast', our Lord once said to his followers, 'do not look gloomy. Rather, be like men on their way to a party. A lowly spirit does not necessarily mean a long face' (Matt. 6.16-18, paraphrased).

In proof of all this, consider two facts:

To begin with, the New Testament, though it has a cross at its very heart, is *basically a book of joy*.

Wherever some Christians have learnt their long faces, they did not learn them there. What is the New Testament's central theme? It is good news, not heavy tidings. These men of the New Testament come bursting in on us crying, 'This is the time the sad earth has been waiting for! The New Age, promised by the prophets, has begun! God has sent his Christ to redeem us from our sins, raised him from the dead, and made us, in him, heirs of everlasting life. Now the Holy Spirit is at work among us, making us cry "Abba, Father", and we exult in hope of heavenly glory.'

When we study the acts of the apostles or read their letters it is the same story. St Paul can sing hymns with his feet in the stocks at Philippi and later, from his Roman prison, write to his converts, 'Rejoice in the Lord always!' St Peter tells us that his persecuted readers in Asia Minor 'rejoice with unutterable and exalted joy'. And the New Testament ends with a Hallelujah chorus 'And they shall reign for ever and ever' and the promise that 'God shall wipe away all tears from their eyes.'

Did these men live a blissful, care-free life? On the contrary, they tell us, again and again, that 'the times are evil'. Nor are they themselves miraculously cushioned against suffering and sorrow. Our Lord himself ends his earthly life on a gibbet. St Paul is a hunted and homeless man who writes 'For thy sake we are killed all the day long; we are counted as sheep for the shambles', and who, in II Corinthians 11, has left such a record of his sufferings for the gospel's sake as, to this very day, evokes our admiring wonder. 'These are they who have passed through great tribulation', says the seer of Patmos concerning the great multitude who are now numbered among the redeemed in the glory of heaven.

Such is the lot and life-style of those who were first called Christians. Are they downcast and despondent? Not a bit of it. They are possessed by that unquenchable serenity in the thick of trouble which makes the New Testament, as James Denney said, 'the most buoyant, exhilarating and joyful book in all the world.'

The second of our facts is this: Down the centuries *the saints have never been sad people*. If they had, they would never have been saints. Two pieces of evidence will suffice.

Rufus Jones the Quaker once asked the famous Roman Catholic layman Baron von Hügel what qualities his church looked for in those whom she canonized as 'saints'. 'Four things', replied the Baron, 'Loyalty to the Faith, heroism in time of testing, power to do the apparently impossible and, fourthly, radiance amindst the storm and stress of life.' Then he added, 'The church may conceivably have been wrong about the first three things, but it is gloriously right about the fourth.'

And here is our second bit of evidence.

William Temple was, by common consent, one of the great Christians of our time. So good and great was the Archbishop that Bernard Shaw called him 'a realized impossibility'. When he died in 1944, a simple countryman who knew him well uttered what might have been his epitaph. Not a word about his fame as thinker or church leader. All he said was, 'William Temple was a very jolly man.'

And might not the same thing be said of all the true servants of Christ whose names never hit the headlines or find their way into the history books? The people who, with something of Christ's own divine compassion, go about befriending the lonely, helping the lame dogs, and bearing other people's burdens – are these usually sad and depressed people? We know that they are not. They are the 'happy warriors' who are too caught up in well-doing to have time to mope and moan over the world's worries and wickedness.

So let us ask, finally: What is the secret of all those radiant people from Paul of Tarsus to Temple of Canterbury? What enables them, 'amid the encircling gloom', to go on their way rejoicing?

We may be sure is not simply natural *joie de vivre*. The secret lies much deeper. It is their belief in God's goodness and their strong certitude of God's final victory over all evil. Whether in the first century or the twentieth, these men and women are sustained by the conviction that God has a great and gracious purpose for his world, a purpose which he is working out amid all the chaos of the present time, a purpose which does not end with death. Such a man was Dr Edward Wilson of Antarctic fame, trapped with his friend Captain Scott in that final, fatal blizzard at the South Pole, and writing thus, from the tent of death, to his wife: 'Don't be unhappy. All is for the best. We are playing a good part in a great scheme arranged by God himself, and all is well.'

This is how they speak, the Christian optimists. Theirs is no fair-weather optimism that has never known 'the cloudy and dark day'. Rather is it what Reinhold Niebuhr called a 'Beyond Tragedy' optimism, the kind of optimism you find in the book of Revelation, the optimism which has looked into the abyss of evil, unaffrighted, because it knows that the world belongs to God and his Christ, and not to the devil.

In other words, *only in the Christian revelation, taken quite seriously, is there firm ground for optimism*. Consult the philosophers, and they will tell you that evil is a 'not-yet', good in the making, something which the onward march of science and progress may be expected to alleviate and dispel. It is a thesis which those of us who have lived through this twentieth century find incredibly hard to accept. Nor can the secular historians give us the clue which we need. For them, all events in history are relative, never final. What they lack is some absolute vantage-point, some commanding position, from which to view the hotchpotch of history.[1] If we mortals are ever to make sense of it, we must have something, or rather Someone, final *in* history as well as *beyond* it.

Now such an absolute vantage-point Christians have in the historic Christ. In what we call the gospel story the End ('End' with a capital E) of history has actually entered history, without ending it in a temporal sense.[2] In the story of the inauguration of God's kingdom in Christ the ultimate meaning of history has been revealed, and in that divine self-disclosure God has given us his master-clue to history. In short, 'the key to history is the historic Christ, above history and in command of it, and there is no other.'[3]

In the atoning cross and its shining sequel we Christians see revealed, in victorious conflict with evil, that holy love of God which still today judges and saves the world.

Christ, God's incarnate Son, crucified for our sins, raised by God's power from the dead, and now reigning with his Father in the unseen world, is the divine solution to the riddle of history.

One day when (please God) we shall sit with our Lord in the heavenly places, the mysteries and tragedies of earth will become plain. We shall see sin and guilt finally destroyed, and, with them, death, darkness and grief. For God's purpose in Christ is nothing less than a moral sovereignty without end, a recreated humanity, and the consummation of all things in a better world than this.

This is Christian faith in its New Testament fulness. This is the faith which, as St John said, 'overcomes the world'.

Notes

1. See D. M. Baillie, *God was in Christ*, Faber & Faber and Scribner's 1948, p. 73.

2. See C. H. Dodd, *The Apostolic Preaching and its Developments*, Appendix, 'Eschatology and Apocalyptic', Hodder & Stoughton 1936, Willett 1937, pp. 193ff.

3. P. T. Forsyth, *The Justification of God*, Duckworth 1916, Scribner's 1917, p. 227.

18

The Christ of Christian Faith

In many lands, from Brazil in the West to New Guinea in the East, the Christian church is very much alive and growing. How different is the situation in Britain, and in other European countries! And as the spiritual flame burns low, our society degenerates. Predictably so: 'Where there is no vision', said the wise man long ago, 'the people perish', (or, more accurately, 'get out of hand', Prov. 29.18, Jerusalem Bible). When Sir Alec Douglas-Home asked Harold Macmillan at what point the rot had set in, that shrewd old man replied, 'When people stopped going regularly to church on Sundays.'[1] Not surprisingly the cynics say that we are now living in 'the post-Christian age'.

Yet, paradoxically, interest in Jesus Christ continues unabated. Between 1910 and 1950 there appeared in the English language alone no fewer than 350 'lives' of Jesus. Since then there have been many more. Nor has interest been confined to the written word. We have only to think of *Godspell* and *Jesus Christ Superstar* to see how he has invaded even the world of show business. Reluctant as Western man may be today to darken a church door, he yet retains a fascinated interest in the Church's Founder.

But mere interest in Christ is one thing, genuine faith in him quite another; and if there is to be a spiritual renaissance in this land, this is the kind of faith we shall need. No 'modernist' belief in Jesus merely as 'the man for others' will do.[2] Our question therefore is: What sort of attitude to Christ deserves the name of full Christian faith?

I

To begin with, it means faith in the *historic* Christ. In English we have two adjectives derived from the word 'history'. 'Historical' means 'having actually happened', whereas 'historic' signifies 'assured of an abiding place in history'. Thus, whatever is known to have happened may be labelled 'historical': only a minority of people (or events) can properly be called 'historic'. Both adjectives are to be applied to Christ. He was, and he abides.

We shall not here discuss the 'historical Jesus'. Only complete cranks and Communists have said that he never existed. Only dyed-in-the-wool sceptics (e.g. Strauss, Bultmann, Hugh Trevor-Roper) have denied that the gospels preserve reliable information about 'the Jesus of history', Jesus as he really was.[3] Our concern is with the 'historic' Christ – with the fact that there was once a Man – a distinct, vivid and quite remarkable person called Jesus – who not only lived and worked and died in Palestine nearly two thousand years ago, but whose power deep in the general heart of man survives to this day:

> That one Face, far from vanish, grows,
> Or decomposes, but to recompose.

Whether we like it or not, Jesus Christ has exerted an influence on history to which there is no real parallel. Out of much evidence let us choose two pieces of unsolicited – and unclerical – testimony.

William Hazlitt recalls how once some of his notable contemporaries fell to discussing 'persons one would like to have met'. When after one great name after another had been mentioned, up got Charles Lamb and said in his stuttering way: 'There is only one other Person. If Shakespeare were to come into this room, we should all rise up to meet him. But if that Person were to come into it, we should all fall down and try to kiss the hem of his garment.'

Or recall what Napoleon said on St Helena to General Bertrand:

Nations pass away; thrones crumble; but the church remains. Whose is the arm which for eighteen hundred years has protected it from the many storms which have threatened to engulf it?

Alexander, Caesar, Charlemagne and myself founded empires. But upon what did we rest the creations of our genius? Upon force. Jesus Christ alone founded his empire upon love; and, at this hour, millions of men would die for him.

So, even in the last quarter of the twentieth century, Jesus Christ continues to command the interest and admiration of men as no other ever born of woman.

Now the faith of people who admire the historic Christ is not a dead faith. Yet, equally, it is not a living one. It is certainly not the faith of Paul, or Peter, or John, or the writer to the Hebrews, or the seer of Patmos; neither has it been the faith of the great Christians down nineteen centuries. Theirs has been faith in one who not merely lived and died, but *is now alive for evermore*.